To Two

have play...
important part of my life.
I pray that you both keep
others for perfection as you
grow spiritcals

Missing Pieces

Finding the Perfect Walk with God

Gwengale Parker

Ithaca Press
3 Kimberly Drive, Suite B
Dryden, New York 13053 USA
www.IthacaPress.com

Cover Design	Gary Hoffman
Book Design	Gary Hoffman

Manufactured in the United States of America

9 8 7 6 5 4 3 2 1

Library of Congress Cataloging-in-Data Available

First Edition

Printed in the United States of America

ISBN 978-0-9825971-5-6

www.GlengaleParker.com

Dedication

To my mother who always speaks the truth to me, no matter how much it hurts. My heart overflows with nothing but love for you. Your godliness and soft-spoken ways, I will always admire.

In Loving Memory of:

My father, Aaron Jones, Sr. and my brother,
Reverend Wendell N. Jones.

TABLE OF CONTENTS

FOREWORD

As we find ourselves living in a society with declining morality, low self esteem, family breakups, lack of family values, teen pregnancies, rising crime rates, and spiritual apathy, I find it extremely refreshing and inspiring to read a book with this title: "Missing Pieces."

I commend and congratulate Rev. Gwengale J. Parker for having the courage and boldness to write this book. It is based on the Word of God, which is the greatest resource available to man. I personally believe that God says what He means and means what He says. "Be ye therefore perfect, even as our Father which is in heaven is perfect." (St. Matthew 5:48) It is written, "Man shall not live by bread alone but by every word that proceeded out of the mouth of God." (St. Matthew 4:4)

I have discovered that our problem with the word "perfect" is in the lack of our willingness to surrender our all to God. The song writer says. "All to Jesus I surrender, All to Him I freely give; I will ever love and trust Him, in His presence daily live." If you surrender your all to God, walking in His perfect Will, in obedience to His Word, the word "perfect" will no longer frighten you or make you feel uncomfortable.

Thank you, Rev. Parker for such an inspiring book. I encourage all to read this book with a spiritual mind; it will certainly change your life. Reading this book has truly been encouraging as well as a blessing to me. Christ so loved the church that He gave Himself for it. That He might sanctify it and cleanse it with the washing of water by the Word. That He might present it to Himself a glorious church, not having a spot or wrinkle, or any such thing, but that it should be Holy and without blemish. (Ephesians 5:25-27)

Jesus is the missing piece...The way to find the perfect walk with God.

To God be the Glory,
Rev. Dr. Ralph M. Cherry

INTRODUCTION

My love for God and the determination to walk in the Word of God in all aspects of my life sometimes leave me feeling as if I live daily among few who feel as I feel. Too many are toying with God's Word, living in sin, justifying their sinfulness by shifting the blame to someone else. There are those who keep on sinning, claiming being human as the reason for their state of confusion and sinfulness. One day I was awakened to a very sad realization, that many proclaiming to know God and believe in Jesus Christ are among the confused who use the Word of God to justify their sinful state of being. They take God's Holy Word, misinterpret the meaning and use the misinterpretation as justification for their wicked ways.

The world is in need of some Christian soldiers, ready and willing to take a stand and live that perfect life that God has commissioned us to live. Christian soldiers who walk in love joy, peace, kindness, long-suffering, gentleness, goodness, faithfulness, and self-control. This is the fruit that Jesus said we must have in order to live that perfect life as we walk with Him.

This is book was written by the directions of God as a revised edition to *"Perfect...Why Not?"* God revealed this to me through one of my hobbies. I love working with puzzles. One day I was feeling up to a real challenge. I chose a puzzle that was quite complex, not in size because it consisted of only 1500 pieces. The complexity was the puzzle itself. In the past I always chose a puzzle filled with bright colors that displayed some type of scenery. This puzzle was different in that there were no bright colors and no scenery. This puzzle was one that was totally black with a streak of light that ran parallel and faded at each end. I remember thinking, "What have I got myself into?" But I am one who doesn't like giving up on anything I start. So I began to tackle the unusual puzzle. The pieces were all similar in that they were black and very close in size.

In order to complete this puzzle and to be sure that every piece was placed in the correct spot. I had to pay close attention to the smallest detail on every piece of the puzzle. Even with the extra care given to each piece there were times when a piece would be out of place. The only way I was able to determine this was by doing a close examination. I would take a flashlight and shine it on the puzzle, it was only then that I could see that a piece was out of place. In our Christian walk it is sometimes necessary to shine a light on our lives so that the missing pieces or misplaced pieces in our lives can be revealed. I used a flashlight to shine on the puzzle which is man-made light. But to do a close examination of our Christian walk we must turn on the supernatural light of Jesus Christ. It is only the light of Jesus that can reveal to us the missing pieces in our lives.

After weeks of working on this puzzle, I was now down to the placement of the last few pieces. The closer I got to what I believed to be the final piece, the more excited I became. I took the last piece from the table in my hand, feeling as if I had accomplished what had appeared to be an impossible task. As I placed what I believed to be the last piece of the puzzle I realized there was a problem. As I looked at the puzzle I realized that what I thought to be the last piece was not the last piece. I believed I was inserting the last piece, but there was a vacant spot. A piece was missing. There was an empty spot that needed to be filled in order to complete the puzzle. So many Christians live their lives thinking that all the pieces are in place, only to find that in the end there is a missing piece or pieces keeping him or her from living the perfect life that God expects of one who accepts Him as their Lord and Savior to live.

God has provided the pieces we are to use in order to live that perfect life as a Christian. But we as Christians or believers must first make a personal decision to strive for perfection.

The purpose of *Missing Pieces* is to relay to Christians as well as non-believers what God expects of us and what pieces we need to make us complete as we strive daily for perfection.

As you read this book I pray that you will open your mind and heart so that you will be able to receive the message in which God wants me to relay to you in this book.

And at the end of the book, understand that you must have a determined mind; determined to be obedient in your walk as you strive daily for completion, as you press on to reach perfection in Jesus Christ.

Chapter One

PERFECTION

*"For all have sinned, and come short
of the glory of God."*

Romans 3:23

Webster's Dictionary defines "perfect" as "thorough; complete or to bring to perfection." There have been times when I have worked tirelessly on a project, paying close attention to the smallest details, in order for the end results to be one of perfection. So often the end results are not perfect, so I have to make changes. Just as we have to make changes in our lifestyle to live as God has commanded us. When we work on projects to be presented to others, we are very particular. A dressmaker will work hard to ensure that a custom dress she has been commissioned to make for a special occasion is a flawless garment. We strive to make material things perfect, but we fall short in our spiritual walk. We make one excuse after another as to why we cannot reach perfection.

When the words "perfect" and "spirituality" are used together, we too often view them as an unattainable goal. Why, do you suppose, if we can connect the word perfect with man-made items, are we not able to connect the word perfect as it pertains to our walk with God? I have watched my husband wash and wax his truck, carefully detailing the tires, and shinning the chrome. When he finishes his detailing, he steps back from the truck to look it over. So often he's said, "Now that's perfect," but the next morning, he can always find a spot he has missed. When we look at our Christian walk can we step back and say that it's perfect? Instead we don't try to make it perfect; we just declare it as an unattainable goal. The good news is that when one decides to walk with God, this walk can be perfect. Just as the dressmaker works hard to please others, and my husband to have a clean truck, we can be perfect in our walk with God. Yes, it takes hard work, but all we have to do is be obedient, study the Word of God, live His Word and strive daily for perfection.

I am often approached by individuals who ask a very familiar question, one that is meant to challenge one's spiritually. "Can a Christian live a sin-free life?" Now, the person asking the question is usually prepared to take a stand against this statement and is armed with the scripture from Romans 3:23 as support:

"For all have sinned, and come short of the glory of God."

Many read this scripture and stop there, failing to read the entire chapter to get the correct understanding. They say, "No, I can't do it. Everyone has sinned, will forever sin and will always come short of God's glory." The first thing we need to note about this scripture is that the scripture says for all *"have sinned."* This means that at some time in our life we sinned, which was done in the past. It does not say that we are sinning and all will keep sinning. Yes, before you were convicted, before you repented and before you confessed with your mouth, you had sinned. But once you accept Jesus Christ as your Lord and Savior, you are no longer a sinner, if you are truly committed to His Holy Word. When you give your life to Jesus Christ, you should be able to stand boldly and say, "I have sinned and at one time fell short of His glory, but I am no longer a sinner. I stand on the Word of God." Declare from this point on to strive daily to reach perfection, but remember first you must arm yourself with wisdom.

I previously stated that perfect is defined as thorough, or complete. In order to understand God's Word we must stop taking portions of the scriptures and using them as a weapon of combat between good and evil. One of the steps toward perfection is to be thorough when reading His Word and get the complete understanding of His Word then apply it in our daily lives. Roman 3:23 does not say that we cannot be perfect, only that at some time or another everyone has fallen short. In the third chapter of Romans, it became apparent to Paul that the Jews did not truly understand the righteousness of God. Because of this realization Paul saw a need to reveal the righteousness of God to the Jews. The Jews were taught and truly believed that everyone who was not Jewish was not good enough to be loved by God. Yes, the Jews were God's chosen people, but now Christ had come and died so that everyone would be saved from their sins. The Jewish nation felt that they would automatically be saved just because of who they were. Just as some of us today believe that we will be saved because of our wealth, and status in society. The Jewish nation believed that it was impossible for the Gentiles to gain righteousness because they were not God's chosen people. Paul assured them that they were no better than the Gentiles. He enlightened them to the fact that because of the sinful nature of man, all men, had sinned and fallen short. But now there is an opportunity for us to live in the present free from sin. This opportunity was extended to us when God sent His beloved Son to die for our sins.

Humans cannot do this alone; we cannot live free from sin simply because we desire to live that way. The sinful nature of man started with Adam and Eve. We can only live free from sin by allowing the guiding hand of Jesus Christ to direct our path. We must never forget that God is a Holy God, a God of truth, a God of love, and it is God who has put in place the requirements or guidelines we need to attain perfection. I believe to say that perfection is unattainable, or to merely question the possibility of living a life of perfection, implies that God is a liar. We must always remember that all things are possible with God. If reaching the goal of perfection is unattainable, God would never make such a demand of His children.

As parents, we expect our children to be obedient. We encourage them to always put their best foot forward and be the best they can be. Through this process we coach them, set guidelines, express expectations and support them as they work to attain their goal. As long as the child is being obedient, working hard, and staying focused we are fine and will not give up on them. Now on the other hand, when they become disobedient, lose their drive to succeed and make excuses we withdraw our support. There are a few parents that can see the results because they walk in faith so they continue to push the child until the goal is reached. Just as the parents who never give up on their children. God never gives up on us, He keeps on protecting, guiding us, and He keeps on pouring out His blessings to us. Even as we make excuses as to why we cannot reach the point of perfection.

I have spent much time searching to understand the mindset of people who proclaim to be Christians, yet refuse to live that true and perfect life God has designed. John 3:16, "For God so loved the world, that He gave His only begotten Son, that whosoever believeth in Him should not perish, but will have everlasting life." Can you even begin to imagine the love God has for us? He loved us so much that He wanted to be sure that He wasn't asking us to do the impossible. He sent His Son to be subjected to all the sins, wickedness and evil ways of this world. His Son Jesus lived a holy life in a sinful world and did not yield to temptation. Through His Son Jesus, God gave us commands that we are to abide by in our daily living; He gave us our guide to perfection. The foundation has been carefully placed on solid ground for us. When we decide to place our feet on the solid ground of Jesus, we stand on assurance. We stand knowing that the ground we now stand on will not buckle to sin, bend to disobedience or bow to corruption or weakness. Standing on the solid foundation of Jesus Christ gives strength and empowers us as soldiers to take a stand to do the will of God. The foundation has been laid, and the pattern of living a Christian life has been given to us through God's Holy

Word. If we abide in His Word, life can only be one of perfection because the perfect pattern has been laid for us by a perfect God.

It is very important that we understand something about our human makeup. The flesh is simply a corruptible covering for a righteous soul. I refer to the flesh as a corrupt covering because the flesh is the reason for spiritual failure. Because of the flesh, we give in to the human desires that cause us to be disobedient, weak, confused and fearful. If we deal with the flesh and not allow it to control, us the flesh can be conquered by a righteous soul. Too often the flesh controls the mindset of an individual causing him or her to fail in their spiritual walk. I am sure by now you are saying the only perfect man to walk this earth was Jesus Christ. Yes, Jesus Christ was the only man, who was fully human and fully divine, a perfect being. The Bible shows us how Jesus was tempted as well as confronted with the evils of this world, but not once did he allow Himself to fall prey to the evil to which he was subjected. Jesus came to earth with a mindset of doing His Father's Will. Jesus did not allow the flesh to get in the way of His Heavenly Father's business.

We must never forget, God is Jesus' Father and He is our Father as well. Since we, as Christians, have the same Father, Jesus is our big brother. When God looks down from Heaven upon each of us, He should not be able to see a difference between us and Jesus. We need to be imitators of our big brother, Jesus.

In order to live and walk as Jesus did we must first have the proper mindset. We should not allow ourselves to be controlled by negative thoughts or influenced by the standards of the world. In fact, we cannot allow society to dictate our standards at all. We must stand on what we believe, and that is the Word of God. We must never get so caught up in the world that we become foolish and forget what God expects of us. He expects us to strive daily to reach perfection.

> *"Are ye so foolish? Having begun in the Spirit: Are ye not made perfect by the flesh?"*
>
> Galatians 3:3

When I think of our foolish ways, I am reminded of the Galatians who first believed with all their hearts in the Holy Spirit. Then they allowed their thoughts to embrace the ideas and teachings of false doctrine. Paul in Galatians 3:3 reminds the Galatians of their beginnings in obtaining salvation, when they believed only in the Holy Spirit, rather than believing that salvation could be obtained through their works and by obeying the laws of the land. The Galatians were diverted from the cross, and caught up in living by the Old Testament laws that were not entirely based on the Holy Spirit.

We are like the Galatians, diverted from the cross, seeking God's glory by abiding by the laws of the land. We must be mindful that the law of the land does not always agree with the law of God. I am not saying that anyone should go out and break the law, but there are laws being put in place that are not God's way. Just because they are laws does not mean it is okay to live them. God is a Holy God, who sent His Holy Son wrapped in flesh to this earth. If it had not been for His Son living Holy in an unholy world, we would all be condemned this day. Jesus did not conform to the ways of the world as He walked on this earth; everything about Him was Holy, including His mind, His will and His emotions. No, we can never live up to the Holiness of Jesus, but we can live and walk in the light of Jesus by putting away the flesh and living the perfect life as Christians as commanded by God, our Heavenly Father.

Don't you think it is time that we, as Christians, take a stand, and be mindful of what we offer God? Why do you suppose we feel that God will accept anything from us? We say we love God and want to be obedient children but we live imperfect lives, mistreating our brothers and sisters, and not living as God has commanded. We keep committing one sin after another, yet, we expect God to keep on handing out blessings. The sad thing about this is that we keep reaching for his blessings knowing we do not deserve them. We need to always take time and thank God for all the blessings He be-stows upon us. It is only because of His grace and mercy that we are continuously blessed. It is only because of His grace that He gives us the gifts of life that we don't deserve. And it is because of His mercy that we are not punished the way we deserve to be for living such sinful lives. How blessed we are, we don't deserve anything He gives us yet He holds back the punishment we do deserve, giving us the opportunity to get it right.

One of my favorite studies of the Old Testament is the different feasts that were celebrated. Many of these celebrations included the offering of sacrifices to God for atonement of the people. During the celebration of Passover, a feast of salvation, lambs were offered as a sacrifice. Not just any lamb, but a special lamb. The finest lamb was hand-picked and examined closely to make sure that the lamb to be scarified was free from spots or blemishes. If anything about the lamb were found to be imperfect the lamb was returned to the herd and the search for the perfect lamb started again. It was of the utmost importance that God was offered nothing less than a perfect lamb. The custom afforded that God would never be offered anything that was less than perfect. I wonder why it is that we, who proclaim to be God-fearing Christians, try to offer God our imperfect lives. After offering our imperfect selves to Him, we expect Him to accept us in our unclean state. I am not referring to when we first give our life to Christ. Because when we first give our life to Christ we come just as we are and allow Him to cleanse us for our Father. We arrive immature looking and longing to be changed. As we progress from immaturity to maturity we strive to advance from immaturity to perfection. God welcomes the opportunity to mold us into that perfect Christian, but we must have the right mindset so that we can stay on the right path.

The beginning of the Christian walk with God begins with many spots and blemishes, as we strive for perfection those spots and blemishes began to fall off of us. A new walk with God should develop into a spotless walk. When the spots come off, they should be removed forever. But first we have to mature as Christians. To become a mature Christian requires total dedication from the time we accept Christ as our Lord and Savior until the day we depart this earthly body.

We are always setting goals for ourselves, career goals, educational goals, financial goals or record breaking goals. We don't mind working hard to reach the goals we have set. We look forward to reaching the goals we set because in the end there is something to be gained. We too must set spiritual goals and strive to reach the goals set by God, because there is a greater reward in the end.

I have talked to many people who have implanted the idea in their minds that no one can ever be perfect, so why should we strive to reach an unattainable goal? First, we must remember this is not a goal set by man, but a goal set by God, a goal that we must strive to reach every day. If you enter into your spiritual walk with a determined mind, then yes, the goal is attainable. God has set the standards, and we, as His children, have an obligation to live up to those standards.

God's Word gives us an account of two men whose lives were described as being perfect, men who have walked this earth, just as you and I do. Let us take a look at the first man whose name was Noah. God described Noah in Genesis 6:9:

> *"These are the generation of Noah: Noah was a just man and perfect in his generations, and Noah walked with God."*

God described Noah as a perfect man. Noah's title as a perfect man of his generation was one to be commended. I believe this because Noah lived during a time of destruction and corruption. Men were busy sinning. Those whom God created were all good, but man corrupted God's way by living as if he had created himself. Violence filled the earth, but there was one who lived as he walked in faith as a perfect man till the end. God's solution to the destruction and corruption of man was to destroy the world. God had the right to make this decision because as the Word tells us, that the earth belongs the Lord and everything on this earth. I believe that when God decided to destroy the world; He just didn't set the plan in motion. He did an evaluation of what was bad on earth and what was good. He looked around, and there was one who lived a perfect life before God and man. God saw Noah, one who did not conform to the world but walked upright. In the mist of sinful times, Noah took a stand against the wrong and lived a righteous life. I know this was not an easy task; ask yourself, can you stand as Noah? Noah, a perfect man in the sight of God, walked with God when everyone else walked in darkness. When you walk with God, you walk alone; no one seems to understand the things you do or say. When God told Noah to build the ark because it was going to rain, he didn't know what to expect because never before had it ever rained on earth. The one thing Noah did know was that God said it, and he believed it, so he acted by putting his faith and trust in God. He acted in obedience to God. If Noah had not been armed with the weapon of a strong mindset, he too would have been caught up in the spirit of darkness. Instead Noah made a choice. He kept his heart, mind and soul on God as he walked with God forsaking all others. Can you look at the life you are living and say without a doubt that if God needed a perfect servant you can stand as Noah stood? Are you a Christian offering God your perfect self, or are you offering him a body covered with the blemishes of adultery, lust, backbiting, lying and selfishness? Yes, we are all aware of Noah's fall after the rain ceased. He became drunk with wine and he lay naked, exposed before his sons. There are many who use this incident to prove that Noah was in no way perfect. And there are many who believe that since there was no account of drunkenness before this account with Noah, believe that Noah was unaware of the side effect wine would have on the body. I personally don't feel this incident is relevant to the fact that Noah was described by God as being a perfect man. If Noah had not been perfect in the sight of God, God would not have described him as being perfect. Noah lived in the mist of corruption and was given the title by God as a perfect man, yet many today proclaim to be Christians, who do not possess the qualities of a Christian. Attending church and bible study regularly and proclaiming righteousness do not gain one the title of perfect.

God was so pleased with Noah, the perfect man, that He made a covenant with Noah. Not just a covenant, but an everlasting covenant.

"And I will establish my covenant with you, neither shall all flesh be cut off any more by the waters of a flood; neither shall there anymore be a flood to destroy the earth. And God

> *said, this is the token covenant which*
> *I make between myself and you and*
> *every living creature that is with you,*
> *for perpetual generations: I set my bow*
> *in the cloud, and it shall be for a to-*
> *ken of a covenant between me and the*
> *earth."*
>
> Genesis 9:11-13

Striving for perfection is a battle that must be fought day by day, hour by hour, minute by minute, second by second. It is one that can be won through Jesus Christ.

Another perfect man, in the sight of God was Job.

> *"And the Lord said unto Satan, Hast*
> *thou considered my servant Job, that*
> *there is none like him in the earth, A*
> *perfect and an upright man, one that*
> *feareth God, and escheweth evil?"*
>
> Job 1:8

Job was a righteous man, who worshipped God and who suffered at the hands of Satan only because God allowed Satan to test Job. The suffering of Job started as the results of a conversation God had with Satan. Just as he is today, Satan was busy searching for someone he could use for his evil works. God asked Satan where he had been. (Satan was free to roam earth and Heaven.) Satan told God that he had

21

been going and coming searching for someone he could corrupt. God asked him if he has considered "his servant" Job, and told Satan that there was none like him on earth. Note: Satan didn't have a need to search out someone that already belonged to him, but someone he could turn against God. God could suggest "His servant" Job, because He knew that Job could stand the test and stand in spite of all the odds against him. Can God allow Satan to use you and know without a doubt that you will stand against all odds? Can you stand when everything is going wrong? Can you stand when all your family and friends turn their backs on you? Can you stand in times of sickness? Can you stand when all your material goods are taken away from you? Can you stand when you lose a loved one? There was one man who could, and God knew this; that's why He called Job "His servant." God explained to Satan that Job was a perfect and upright man, who feared God and stayed away from evil. God allowed Satan to use Job because God knew that Job was a righteous man, who would remain faithful even when it seemed to him that God had left him.

Where do you turn when it seems like God has left you? Do you turn to worldly means or do you stand on the promise of God? Do you stand knowing that God has promised never to leave you or forsake you? God had taken me though some times in my life, but no matter how hard things got, no matter how heavy my burden got, I kept on standing, and I will keep on standing. I stand alone because my friends and family don't understand the choice I made to live a righteous life. But I made up in my mind a long time ago that I will stand just as Job stood. No matter what trials and tribulations come into my life, no matter how heavy the burdens on my shoulders become. I will not break but will continue to stand on the promises of God. Yes, no matter what I face daily, I will continue to strive for perfection.

Job was given the title of "My servant." To be addressed as "GOD'S SERVANT" is an honor far above any title we can earn. God knew there was no doubt about who Job served. He had seen Job stand for righteousness when no other would, and He had heard Job praying night and day for his family. He saw Job giving thanks in all things, and taking a stand against the evils of the world. Therefore God had no problem allowing Satan to test Job, because He knew that Job was a man who would not bend or break in times of trials and tribulations. Job, God's servant, would not allow himself to be corrupted by Satan. Satan couldn't see what God could see so he was determined to prove God wrong. Satan told God that the only reason Job was remaining faithful to him was because of the things He had blessed Job with. In other words Satan was saying, "God, if you take away all his material possessions, he would be like everyone else. He would turn away from you." Satan believed that Job would only serve God as long as he was being blessed with material gain. But God knew Job's heart; He gave Satan permission to take away all of Job's worldly possessions. But the one thing God would not allow Satan to touch was Job's soul. God allowed Satan to strip Job of all his worldly goods so that Satan and the world would be reminded of the sovereignty of God. He also needed to see that Job loved God because of who God was and not for the presents He had given him. We, as Christians, need to stop asking God for presents and thank Him for allowing us to enter into His presence and in all things give Him the glory.

Job never complained. Instead, he tore his robe and fell face down on the ground and worshipped God in spite of his despair. The torn robe symbolized Job's hurt and shock. He shaved his head, symbolizing the loss of his personal glory. When he did these things Job said, "I am deeply saddened but I will continue to praise and worship you in all things. How do we know that Job continued to worship God? When he fell to the ground Job looked up toward Heaven and said:

> *"Naked came I out of my mother's womb and naked shall I return thither: the Lord gave and the Lord hath taken away; blessed be the name of the Lord."*
>
> Job 1:21

Job stood steadfast because he knew what he believed and who he believed in. We miss the mark of perfection because we say with our mouths that we believe and trust in God with all our heart, but when times get tough, we start complaining. We complain about our situation and stop praising and worshipping God. Why is this? This is because we worship God according to the blessings He bestows upon us. We try bargaining with God; if you bless me I will worship you. But when we receive the blessings we stop worshipping Him. How foolish we are to believe for one minute that we can bargain with God. There is no bargaining with God. It is He who has all power in His hands not us.

Only a perfect man could have endured the pain and suffering that Job endured. Job kept his eyes lifted up toward Heaven because he was armed with the weapon of a strong mindset to be perfect in the sight of his Heavenly Father. Job stood when his friends and loved ones turned their backs on him. Job continued to stand when his wife encouraged him to curse God and die. He stood even as he sat in the garbage dump with his body covered with sores. We too can stand through all things if we keep our mind on Jesus. I am not saying that Job didn't get weary along the way, but in his weariness he knew who to continue to call on. He never took his eyes off the prize.

Noah and Job did not allow the sinful ways of the world, or their flesh to stand in the way when it came to living the perfect life as commanded by God. I'm sure they too were faced with the same temptations that we face today. But we cannot be led by what looks good and feel good to the flesh. We cannot afford to live by what society says is acceptable, if God says it's a sin it is a sin.

In the fifth chapter in of the book of Matthew, beginning with the twenty-first verse, Jesus is teaching his disciples what our Father expects of us and the way to attain righteousness. Jesus realized that somewhere along the way we would lose focus and become confused about what God expects of us. In looking at this chapter Jesus said many times, "Ye have heard that it was said," and he goes on to say, "But I say unto you," Jesus is reminding us that the ways of God are not what man says they are nor what we have heard from other sources. God's Word is to be taken the way He meant it with no additions and nothing taken away. After Jesus had completed clarifying the Word of God, He ended with:

"Be ye therefore perfect, even as you
Father which is in heaven are perfect."
Matthew 5:48

How can we as Christians believe in God's Holy Word that we know to be true, and still tell ourselves we cannot be perfect? No, we will never reach perfection as long as we never make an effort to strive for perfection. When one takes on the determination to strive for perfection, he or she must be ready to endure the suffering just as Jesus Christ.

Striving for perfection means one must always display the fruit of the spirit, love, joy, peace, patience, kindness, goodness, faithfulness, gentleness, self-control and long-suffering. Perfection means we must first peel off the flesh. This is done by removing the old self and putting on the new self.

> *"Lie not one to another, seeing that*
> *ye have put off the old man with his*
> *deeds; And have put on the new man,*
> *which is renewed in knowledge after*
> *the image of him that created him."*
>
> Colossians 3:9-10

Once the old self has been removed it is then we can begin to set goals on how to reach the point of perfection.

> *"Be ye therefore followers of God, as*
> *dear children; And walk in love, as*
> *Christ also hath loved us, and hath*
> *given himself for us an offering and*
> *a sacrifice to God for a sweetsmelling*
> *savour."*
>
> Ephesians 5:1-2

Let us make a new start, and clear our minds, and hearts from all the negative thoughts that have been instilled in us. We must begin to strive to live as God would have us live, by being obedient children. If we follow his pattern we can't go wrong. As we begin anew on this long journey, we must remember, this journey here on Earth is all about God and has nothing to do with us.

WHY NOT BE PERFECT?

decisio
to de
pe

Chapter Tw

MISSING PIECES

W hy do we believe that living a perfect life in Christ is impossible? Is it because we are so concerned about what society says is right or wrong? Or is it the fear of being different? There seems to be a misconception in understanding what we must do to receive the gift of eternal life. As Christians, we need to understand that we must do more than profess that we are Christians; we must have some things in place. These things must be in place if we expect to receive the gift of eternal life. First, we must understand that just because we were created by God and we belong to Him does not mean we don't have to do anything to receive His gift. We have got to be obedient, study His Word; we must put aside all foolishness and understand that our soul salvation is a very serious issue. Where we spend eternity is a

made by individuals, this has nothing
with anyone else. Therefore, striving for
rfection is a personal affair, a personal decision that only you can make for yourself.

*"Now, the works of the flesh are mani-
fest, which are these, adultery, fornication, uncleanness, lasciviousness,
idolatry, witchcraft, hatred, variance,
emulations, wrath, strife, seditions,
heresies, envying, murders, drunkenness, reveling, and such like: of the
which I tell you before, as I have also
told you in time past, that they which
do such things shall not inherit the
kingdom of God."*

Galatians 5:19-21

Whenever I am working on a puzzle the
first thing I do is lay out all the pieces.

I place all the pieces face up on the table
where I will be working with the puzzle. Laying
out all the pieces allow me to see just what I
have to work with. While preparing to put together the unusual puzzle I previously described,
a piece was missing, which means the puzzle
was incomplete. I quickly realized that unless
I found the missing piece, the puzzle would
never be perfect. Also, if I had not put all the
pieces in place I would have never known that I
was one piece from having a completed puzzle.
The same applies to how we go about determin-

ing the piece or pieces in one's spiritual life that are missing. First we open God's Word to gather the knowledge or the pieces that God requires. Once we have an understanding of what God requires it is then that we lay out the pieces so that we can start putting them into their prospective places. Because of our human makeup, unlike the puzzle I was putting together, there may be some pieces already filling some of the spots. These pieces will need to be moved and replaced with the pieces you will lay out. Some may need to move strife, seditions, drunkenness, drug abuse, unclean language, lasciviousness and the inability to forgive and forget the past. When these things are removed, the right pieces can be perfectly placed.

As you are laying out the pieces, do so paying close attention to each piece. The pieces: love, joy, peace, kindness, meekness, gentleness, faith, trust, commitment, goodness, patience, endurance, understanding, hope, long-suffering, praise, thanksgiving, truth, prayer and armor. As you look at the pieces that are laid out, first decide what pieces in your life need to be removed. I am referring to the pieces that have been in the wrong place for a long time. They are the imperfect pieces that must be removed in order for you to strive for perfection. Some may need to remove the piece of adultery. Some may need to remove more than one piece, maybe fornication, lying, cheating, backbiting, and hatred. Some may need to remove the pieces of envying, jealousy, wrath, and idolatry.

I became interested in the hobby of putting together puzzles at a young age, and have completed many puzzles. There is one thing I have never encountered when putting together a puzzle. I have never been able to fit two pieces in one spot. Nor have I ever been able to place one piece on top of another. In order to put the right pieces in place there must to be an empty space available. There is no way that we can keep junk in our heart and mind and cover it by overlaying the correct piece. When a new piece is laid over the old piece you are simply covering up the old piece that can be uncovered at any given time. This indicates that you are not ready to change, so you cover up the wrong pieces in order to look good to others. There have been occasions when I come across a puzzle that I am especially partial. When this happens, I prepare it to be framed. I glue the puzzle pieces to a board to ensure the pieces will not come apart. When we put the pieces of life together we need to ensure the pieces are glued together. The pieces must be held together with the strongest glue. It is then we are assured that no matter how we are tossed about the pieces will remain linked together.

We make many decisions in our life, one being the choice of two lifestyles. The first lifestyle choice is one that derives from society and what feels good to the flesh. For instances, society would have us believe it's alright to commit adultery as long as no one involved is hurt. It is a normal reaction to show hatred to someone who has wronged you. Drunkenness is just a part of being sociable. Society would also lead us to believe that backbiting is fine when you are climbing the ladder of success. Lasciviousness is the good life, so ahead, be wasteful if you can afford it. Paul, in the book of Galatians, warns us against all that strives on evil. We are warned against the sins of the flesh. If anyone walks in these things they will not inherit the kingdom of God. The second lifestyle choice is the decision to live a life walking in the light of God. Striving daily for perfection, not living life based on flesh. The ways of man are destined to lead you down a road of destruction. The ways of God will lead you to eternal life.

When all the pieces of the puzzle are laid out, I then began to work on the border or the outer edge of the puzzle. When putting a puzzle together, there must be boundaries. Boundaries establish a starting point. Having a starting point gives me something to build on. In our Christian walk it is the boundaries that establish where we walk. The boundaries are the building point for our relationship with God. There is nothing outside of the boundaries that connects us to God. It is the boundaries of the puzzle that keeps me within the reach of completing the puzzle. In our Christian walk, boundaries keep us within the reach of God as we strive for perfection. Having boundaries is important because this is the foundation in our spiritual realm. It is the border or foundation that serves the purpose of keeping our mind within the perimeter of living a spirit-filled life while striving for completion in the struggle to reach perfection.

When I discovered a piece of the puzzle was missing, I became very upset. I believed I was near the end of something I had worked so hard to complete. I remembered the hard work and time I had put into this project, only to discover that it would never be complete. Before I gave up, and accepted the incomplete puzzle, I got down on my hands and knees and searched high and low the missing piece. The first day I could not find the piece so I stopped looking. The next day I decided to look again. This time I did something different. I use a flashlight to shine under the table and sofa to make sure I hadn't overlooked the piece. Using the flashlight paid off, I found the piece under the sofa. Even though I had looked the day before in the same area, I had missed it. It wasn't until the next day, as I walked by the puzzle on the table, I stopped and looked at it, totally disgusted with the final outcome. It was then, I felt as if I had given up my search for the missing piece to soon, so I began to search again. I needed to find the missing piece because I was determined to have a completed puzzle. Once again I got on the floor on my hands and knees making a final attempt to find the missing piece. I turned on a light. It was the light that allowed me to see the missing piece.

As Christians, we must get it right. Sometimes we give up to easy, accepting the fate of being lost, because man has implanted this in our mind. Man says no one can change, and no one can ever live a life of perfection. But we must grasp a determined mindset to get it right. Once you have the determination to insert the right pieces in the right places, you can then start searching the heart. Searching for the piece or pieces needed for you to begin your new walk, striving for perfection. You may have to get on your hands and knees. You may even have to lay flat on your face. With God as your guide, you can find those missing pieces. Don't forget to turn on the light when you start searching. It is only the light of God that can open your heart. With an open heart you will be able to recognize the piece or pieces needing to be replaced.

Chapter Three

LAY OUT THE PIECES

The missing pieces in the lives of many are the reason for failed relationships; the inability to love; as well as the inability to forgive. Missing pieces are the reason families are torn apart and filled with envy and hatred for one another. Missing pieces are the reason for broken homes. The lack of love from a father is the reason that daughter seeks love elsewhere. And yes, missing pieces is the reason why many sisters and brothers in Christ work against one another, causing strife in the church. Missing pieces makes us weak. When we are weak we are unable to take a stand against the evils of this world. It is in our weak state that we give in to the ways of the world.

When there are missing pieces in our life, we are like a sand castle built on the beach shore.

Sand castles are usually built on the beach near the water. The reason being is that the wet sand is used to hold the sand castle together. No matter how beautiful the sand castle may be when the tide comes in it is washed away, just as in our lives when pieces are missing. We may look good as long as no trials come into our life, but when we are tested by the world, the tide washes us away. It is then that we allow ourselves to be controlled by the ways of the world. The missing piece in both situations is the foundation. We must not allow this to continue to happen in our life. We must fill those empty spaces or replace the pieces in those spots. Whether you are filling the space or replacing a piece, you must be careful. It's important that the pieces are placed in order to start building a strong foundation. It's time that we put aside self, as well as the ways of the world, and strive to live according to God's Holy Word. It's time to take a close look at the flaws in your life, and replace the piece that is keeping you from attaining the goal of completion. God promised us a life filled with peace and blessings, but first we must be obedient children and put the pieces in the right place. The first piece in place must be the piece of obedience. It is the piece of obedience that all the other pieces hinge from. We all can live a perfect life in Christ if all the pieces are in place. It's time to lay out the pieces so that we can get started putting everything in it prospective place.

Laying out the pieces means there is a need for conviction. When a person is convicted, he or she realizes that there are things in their life that are contrary to God's Holy Word. Once a person is convicted, he or she then repents and accepts Jesus as his Lord and Savior. It is then that he or she begins to put the pieces in place. The believer, on the other hand, has a very hard time with conviction. Because for a long time, the believers with missing pieces have spent a lifetime attending church; believing they are complete in their walk with God. But once the pieces are laid out they realize there are some missing pieces and their walk with God was not what they believed it to be. A time must come in everyone's life when we are forced to take a long hard look in the mirror. Taking a close look in the mirror will reveal that there are missing pieces and empty spots that need to be filled. Or there may be some pieces that are in the wrong spot that need to be rearranged. The pieces that are in the wrong spot are the things in our life that are almost right but need some fine tuning. In order to fine tune our lives we must first understand how God wants us to be. God desires for us to be useful vessels, wholesome and filled with His spirit.

God gave Jeremiah a close look at the work of a potter, as he made a pot. This close look was symbolic of how God reshapes each of us for His perfect works as we prepare for perfection.

*"The word which came to Jeremiah
from the Lord, saying, Arise, and go
down to the potter's house, and there
I will cause you to hear my words.
Then, I went down to the potter's
house, and behold, he wrought a work
on the wheels. And the vessel that he
made of clay was marred in the hand
of the Potter, so he made it again, into
another vessel, as seemed good to the
potter to make it. Then the Word of
the Lord came to me, saying, O house
of Israel, cannot I do with you as this
potter? saith the Lord. Behold, as the
clay is in the potter's hand, so are ye
in mine hand, O house of Israel."*

Jeremiah 18:1-6

No matter how long you have been on this spiritual journey there is always a need to take a close look at yourself, a moment to check and see if there are any missing pieces in your spiritual life. In the scriptures above, God directed Jeremiah to go to the potter's house and observe the work of the potter. God sent Jeremiah to the potter's house. He sent him so that he would get a visual image of the message he needed to relate to a nation. God has the same message for us in our spiritual walk. Now, notice God didn't tell Jeremiah to go to the potter's house for him to tell the potter how to make a pot. Nor did God send him to make suggestions to the potter on how to make a better pot. God has given us the guidelines on how we are to live. But we are constantly offering God suggestions on how we think we should live. There comes a time when we must do as Jeremiah, observe. We are sometimes so busy looking that we can't see for looking. Stop and see as you allow God to make you over as He sees fit.

God told Jeremiah to arise and go to the potter's house. The first thing we need to note about Jeremiah; when God gave him these directives is that he was obedient. He didn't make excuses, but he got up and went to the potter's house as soon as he received the message from God. If we are to be what God wants us to be we must first be obedient and not hesitate to do what He tells us what He wants us to do. What did Jeremiah see at the potter's house? Let us take a trip to the potter's house and get a glimpse of what Jeremiah saw so that we can better understand the message God was relating to Jeremiah, that we too need to understand.

When Jeremiah got to the potter's house he saw a potter sitting at the potter's wheel, making a pot. Before the potter began to make the pot, he started with a mixture of clay and water. The clay and water mixture was then taken to the wheel where it was spun until it took the shape of a vessel. Jeremiah observed the potter at the wheel molding the clay into a pot. But then the potter took the incomplete vessel from the wheel and marred it. The pot wasn't the perfect pot. The potter being dissatisfied tore the vessel apart and started the process over again. It's amazing how the potter never made two vessels alike. But the end results of all the vessels were the same. They all had to be useful vessels. Each vessel was unique, but all were useful vessels. All made with a purpose for a special purpose by the same potter.

God is the Master Potter of all potters. And we are the clay in His hand being formed into perfect vessels. Our beginning was clay in the Master's Hands the day He scooped up a handful of dirt and said, "I'll make me a man." The Master Potter shaped each of us to be the perfect image of Him by breathing the breath of life into us. There are times when the dirt tries to rise above the Hands that made us. It is then the Master Potter tears us down, and makes us over. He makes us over until we understand that we are His. And we are to be what He wants us to be, not what we want to be. Jesus told us that we are to be perfect just as our Father who lives in heaven. When we as His children offer Him anything less than our perfect selves, He tears us down and starts the remaking process. The tearing down process may come through sickness, financial hardships, unemployment, the loss of a loved one or any life changes. It's during these struggles that we are more apt to become concern and question what pieces may be missing in our life.

The Master Potter does not want or need a useless vessel, a vessel that leans instead of standing tall. He does not want or need a vessel with a crack just below the rim. A crack in this position means that just when God begins to see a perfect, useful vessel one filled with the Holy Spirit, sin began to slowly creep in and the Holy Spirit leaks out. God surely can't use a vessel that is missing a piece of pieces from the sides. This means that this vessel can only be used by the world, allowing sin to camp inside the vessel. Where there is sin the Holy Spirit cannot dwell. Sin in the broken vessel pushes out the Holy Spirit. The tearing down process forces us to lay out the pieces and determine what needs to be eliminated or added to our life. Adding the right pieces, the pieces supplied by God, is what gives us that strength to strive for that perfect life as a Christian. Yes, with God's help through His Son Jesus Christ, we can live a perfect life.

By now you may be asking the question, how do I go about finding the missing pieces my life? Well, first you must open your heart and mind and recognize God for who He is, and know without a doubt that He is your Creator and your being rest only in His Hands. And understand that no one on this earth can or have the ability to love you the way God loves you. After all, do you know of anyone who would allow their only child to die for the wrong doings of others? God allowed His Son to die for our sins, Jesus had done no wrong, but He did it for you.

> *"For God so loved the world that he gave His only begotten Son, that whosoever believeth in him should not perish, but have everlasting life."*
>
> John 3:16

> *"But he was wounded for our transgressions; he was bruised for our iniquities: the chastisement of our peace was upon him; and with his stripes we are healed."*
>
> Isaiah 53:5

We must believe in God, and accept Jesus Christ as our Lord and Savior. Accepting is the beginning of building a relationship with Him. Once a relationship has been established, it is then because the light has been turned on in our hearts, we can see who we really are. When the light is on we can see the missing pieces in our life. Yes, the light of Jesus must be turned on before you can see the real you. I don't know of anyone who looks in a mirror in the dark, they always turn on a light. Darkness is very deceitful. In the dark, wrong appears to look right. In the dark sinful ways are justified. But it is the light that reveals our true inner self, a broken vessel with missing pieces.

In order for us as vessels of God to be whole and useful we must carefully lay out each piece, being very careful not to overlook one. Lay out the piece of love, what does love look like in your life? Lay out the piece of peace, are you at peace at all times or is your life one of confusion? Do you have joy all the time or just when things are going your way? What about long-suffering, gentleness, goodness, faith, meekness and temperance? Take a close look at all of these, because they are the pieces that bind so many pieces together. They bind together the missing links. Do you know what's missing in your life? What piece or pieces are keeping you from living that perfect life? It is the piece commissioned by Jesus Christ as the way to obtain righteous living. Please realize this is an examination of you and you alone. It's not about someone else and God but you and God. Too often we try to justify our sinful ways based on the life of someone else or others. You have got to forget about others and take a personal look at your life. When judgment day comes you will be judged by the way you lived not the way anyone else has lived his or her life. It is through your relationship with Jesus Christ that the missing pieces in your life can be revealed to you.

Once you have identified the missing pieces, pick each up one at a time and ask your Heavenly Father to direct you in placing each piece in their rightful place.

Chapter Four

LIVING IN BONDAGE

We as a people are being held captive. The sad thing about this statement is that we are so caught up and bound with the desires of the flesh that we are blind to reality. The human flesh places in our spirit the need for fleshly satisfaction that too often penetrates our mind, heart and soul. Once the fleshly desired have penetrated the mind, heart and soul, we began to operate out of emotions. To be emotionally satisfied means we have conquered our desires or have attained whatever we feel we need to make us feel good. Allowing our fleshly desire to become our driving force is what opens us up for sin to take control of us.

Sin has the ability to control us just because we like what we are doing, it feels good and it's fun. Daily we are faced with situations that we usually dismiss with the idea of that's how things are in the world today. We are surrounded by the bond of sin; it's in our commute to work, in the workplace, in our daily conversations with family and friends. What God wants and needs are those who are willing to stand strong; willing to stand on what His Word teaches and those that are willing to walk daily in love. A Christian or believer should know in his heart that God is God, the great I AM and that Jesus Christ is our Lord and Savior. Believing this empowers us to live and walk as Jesus Christ did. I describe sin as being the foolishness of man in action. In Proverbs, we are told that a man who does not acquire wisdom is a foolish man. Wisdom, as described in the book of Proverbs, does not refer to the amount of education a person has, nor his status in the business community. It is the wisdom given to us by God. A wise man does not allow his self to be bounded by fleshly desires, but only the word of God.

As a child I loved playing outside. I often played cowboys and Indians with my siblings. The goal was for the cowboys or the Indians to capture each other. Once captured, the bad guy's hands and feet were tied to keep them from escaping. No one liked being the one who was captured because no one liked the idea of being tied up. When the hands and feet are tied movement is restricted. I can remember getting captured and tied up, I would struggle hard to break free. Freedom meant being able to do what I needed to for myself and not being restricted. When a person is bound, he or she is at the mercy of whomever or whatever binds them. When I was captured I would beg to be freed because I could not deal with being confined and restricted. This is what happens when one lives in sin. Sin is a very strong bonding agent; it restricts our ability to serve God. We were created by God for the purpose of serving Him, by serving others. It's impossible to serve God and others if we are living in bondage. We have got to break the chain that binds us. Just as a chain has many links, there may be many links in the chains that bind you. But no matter how many links there are in your chains, the stronghold they have over you can be broken. They can only be broken by way of Jesus Christ.

Usually, when we think of being held in bondage we think of someone in prison, or being tied up and held against their will. There are two types of bondage, physical bondage and mental bondage. Physical bondage is being held in a confined area against your will, or imprisoned for wrong doings. A person who is physically bounded has no control over his/her ability to move about, nor are they free to do the things they most enjoy. They are at the mercy of someone else at all times, for example a person in prison cannot decide when he/she wants to eat this is decided for them. They are not allowed to do anything without permission. Usually a person who is physically bounded in most situations was imprisoned because of some wrong doings. Many wrongful acts can be associated directly to another type of bondage, known as mental bondage. Our mind is what controls us and leads us to our destiny. The mindset sets the standards of how we treat others. The mind is also what controls our ability to love or allow ourselves to be loved. Unlike physical bondage where an individual has no control over a situation; mental bondage is something an individual can control if they chose to. Usually mental bondage occurs when someone has been forced to endure things in their life that has been inflicted on them by others. Mental bondage is the end results of an abused child, abusive relationship and a broken home. These deep rooted feelings can hold an individual captive and damage their entire life. Yes, mental bondage can be overcome. It is just a matter of the individual taking control of their mindset. This in term changes the way one looks at a certain situation. The desire to be free from whatever binds us, and the ability to accept freedom can come only by the way of Jesus Christ. Being loosed begins with a change in the mindset.

> *"Set your affection on things above,*
> *not on things on the earth."*
>
> Colossians 3:2

Physical bondage and mental bondage sometimes join forces causing adversity within an individual. Physical bondage affects a person's thoughts and actions. When a person is held in physical bondage for a period of time and set free; they harvests unnatural feelings in the mind causing them to react in an unpredictable manner. They live life based on emotions which forces them to give in to the ways of the world. It's important that we understand, being held in bondage physically and mentally does not mean a person have to remain in this state. God's Word tells us to set our mind on God and not on things on the earth. The perfect formula, there is no way anyone can live in bondage and in Jesus Christ. A choice must be made, to live a life entangled in the calamity of this world; or a life of freedom through Jesus Christ. God does not force us to choose Him. But, if the correct pieces are in place, there is no problem when it comes to making the right decision.

Who lives in bondage? Children who live in bondage grow up to be adults who live in bondage. A child raised in an abusive home, verbally and physically. Always belittled, never receiving any encouragement from his or her parents. The household is a catastrophe, leaving the child totally confused on the differences in right and wrong. A child that is unable to grow and mature in a normal way because he or she is forced to live as an adult at a very early age. The physical and mental abuse inflicted on any child, causes an emotional eruption that fuels the spirit of hatred and un-forgiveness, untrusting and the inability to love or to allow anyone to love him or her. Too often the adults entrusted by God to care for children have chained them in bondage. Being held captive is the reason for a lack of compassion and a harden heart. This type of behavior is passed from generation to generation because no one is willing to take a stand and break the chains of bondage. This forces future generations to live with the missing piece of love. This is also the beginning of generational curses, passed from one generation to another.

> "But the fruit of the Spirit is love, joy, peace, longsuffering, gentleness, goodness, faith, meekness, temperance: against such there is no law. And they that are Christ's have crucified the flesh with the affections and lusts. If we live in the Spirit, let us also walk in the Spirit. Let us not be desirous of Cain glory, provoking one another, envying one another."
>
> Galatians 5:22-26

Being held in the bondage forces a person to seek out the things that appeals only to the flesh, or what makes them feel good. When the missing piece is love, one does not know what love is. Therefore when someone ties to reach out in love they reject the one that is reaching out. This person also lacks the ability to give love. They spend their time searching for love in the wrong places. They seek love in abusive relationships. They believe being beaten every-day is the way they are shown love. A young woman who grows up with no father, or posi-tive role male role model, believes that love is going from man to man, fulfilling her needs based on the flesh and emotions. Because she has never known the love of a caring father, she does not understand the love and respect she should receive in a relationship. Not knowing what true love is all about, she search for what feels good to her at that moment. No one in this position will ever find true love, until they are able to understand that God is Love; and it is He who has set the standards and defined what love is. If a person fails to seek God, he or she will never know true love. God's Word tells us that "God is Love" so unless one seeks Him first they will never know what it is to love or be loved.

My heart is especially sad for the young ladies who spend most of their lives looking for love. Because they don't have a true under-standing of love, their life is full of one heart breaking experience after another. The fear of loneliness drives them from one man to anoth-er, giving birthed to unwanted children. Not only is this young lady living in bondage, but she teaches her children to live in bondage. Will the children ever come to know how to love or will they continue the curse of bondage as they follow in their mother's footsteps?

Will that young girl ever know how to love after she has been sexually abused by her mother's live in boyfriend or that relentless family member? Or will the young man ever know how to love after being forced to engage in unnatural sexual acts with his mother's boyfriend or a ruthless family friend? Our children deserve so much more than what's being offered to them. Children can only be taught to love by adults, but in order to be examples for our youth we as adults must first break free from the sinful acts that bind us and trickle down to our children. It is the lack of love that allows that father or mother to walk away from the family. It is the lack of love that allows us to use and abuse others. It is the lack of love that allows people to stand by and watch someone being murdered and not call for help. It is from the lack of love that a young man can drive by and shoot an innocent person as they walk down the street. The lack of love is the reason youth mistreat and disrespect their elders. We must put the missing piece of love in place for a wholesome life by removing self for the equation. Selflessness brews loveless individuals.

The drug addict is one who is bounded with the lack of peace, joy and self-control. This is one who depends on a substance, to give them a temporary escape from life's reality. When one is high on drugs, the mind tricks the addict into believing that this place supersedes all places. The mind is what controls all of our action as well as what we believe to be right or wrong. We must control the mind, because it is the seat of the soul, whatever sits there is what you become. There is a process that takes place when the mind is not controlled. The mind is the place where the flesh brews it feelings, then the inner self or the spirit within you merge. Once the mind and inner self links together, the end results are the belief and lifestyle of the world; and this is who that person becomes. In other words, whatever idea is embedded in the mind, the spirit within you will either confirm the idea or sway the mind away from the thoughts. If one harvests evil thoughts in the mind about a situation that has affected his or her life; the thoughts of the mind soon enters in the spirit and the emotions. These emotions allow the flesh to take control, when this happen the person then lives in bondage to evil thoughts.

There are so many living in the bondage of un-forgiveness. It is un-forgiveness that turns daughters against mothers, sons against fathers, wives against husbands and Christians against fellow brothers and sisters. I am often asked the questions: What's happening to families? Why is there division in the family? The inability to forgive is the major problem within families. I am sure that if given the opportunity to closely examine the reasons for a broken family the findings would be un-forgiveness. Un-forgiveness is the usual type of bondage because when someone lives in un-forgiveness the mind leads that person to believe that their inability to forgive is hurting the person who they feel has wronged them. When in reality un-forgiveness really holds the one who is unwilling to forgive in bondage. When someone refuses to forgive someone they are the ones who has no peace of mind, are not free to know the joys of life. Their mind is always engaging in thoughts of getting even, and the fear of seeing that person. And not only does the inability to forgive takes away the peace and joy of live, but affects the way they handles relationships with others.

This chapter is not to deal with the solutions, but to allow you to take a close look at the issues we face daily. It is meant to turn on the light in our heart so that the issues that are usually swept under the rug are exposed. We see things that are not right, and know in our heart they are not right, but as long as they are not uncovered we continue to pretend they do not exist. It is time for us to stop making excuses for what we believe to be irresolvable issues and search for the underlying problem. The beginning of all problems that is deep within a person is because the person is chained in some type of bondage. The chains can be broken because the Word of God ensures us that "I can do

all things through Christ who strengthens me."
(Philippians 4:13)

The ministry that God has called me unto
has afforded me the opportunity to witness to
many hurting young men and women. All of
them had something in common; their hurt
disappointments and inability to function as
adults stem from being scarred by a dysfunction-
al childhood. Parents as well as family members
are the source for so much pain and hurt in the
young adults. Imparting in them the spirit of
un-forgiveness; rebellion; selfishness; the spirit
of lust and hatred; all in the name of so called
love. It's time to break the generational curses,
it is time God's people step forward and make a
difference.

I encountered two very unique situations
where a young lady was being held captive by
her mother because of her mothers' past lifestyle. The mother of this young lady was very
controlling. She harvested hatred in her heart
for her mother, father and other family members. The hatred was so strong that she isolated
herself from her family and anyone who did
not agree with her or her lifestyle. She was constantly in and out of one meaningless relationship after another. She confused the need to
control with love when it came to her daughter.
The young lady did not have the opportunity
to live the life of a normal teenager. She was
not allowed to have friends unless there were
associates of her mothers' children. She was not

allowed to talk on the telephone or go out with friends to a movie. She was a prisoner in her own home. She was introduced to one daddy after another, but not allowed to have a relationship with her biological father. Finally, one day the young lady took a stand against her mother's ways. She demanded that she be allowed to have a relationship with her father. It was then that her mother gave her a choice, to live in her house or have a relationship with her father. When the young lady made the decision to spend a weekend with her father her mother abandon her. The mother made it clear to her daughter that she had to choose which parent she wanted to have a relationship with. Having a relationship with both parents was not an option. At the age of sixteen the young lady faced depression, disappointment, and abandonment. The young lady's hurt was not only inflicted by her mother but her father's inability to establish a relationship with his daughter as well. The choices made by her parents, and the inability of the parents to put selfishness aside could have damaged her for life. But God didn't allow that to happen. He placed her around people that gave her the opportunity to live as a teenager and taught her about forgiveness. Because the young lady sought a new mindset, she now walks in love and forgiveness as she strives for success.

Another example of walking in forgiveness is a young man who was raised in a Christian home, and knew God. He was taught how to love and the Word of God. But he turned his mind to the world. He became entangled with the idea of gaining material goods and turned from God. Not choosing his friends carefully landed him in prison. He was set up by people he believed to be his friends, accused and convicted because of the choice he made. He tried to blame everyone else for his decision. He lived for a long time with hatred in his heart for the so-called friends who set him up. He finally realized that the choice he made was his choice. He finally asked God to forgive the people that put him in prison, and accepted that he had to pay for the choice he made. He has now forgiven the people that changed his life. He lives everyday striving for perfection.

The time is now! We must break the chains that bind us. It's time to break the chains of unforgiveness, selfishness, unrighteousness, living in the past, unfaithfulness, and the inability to love. Break the chains of lust, material gain, lying, cheating, stealing, and drug addiction. We must let go of physical and mental abuse and the worshipping of false gods. It's time now to live the life God expects of us. God sent us a message through His Son Jesus, "Be ye perfect as my Father is in heaven" (Matthew 5:48). It's time to take the message seriously, but first we have got to break the chains that bind us. It can be done through Jesus Christ, because through him all things are possible.

Chapter Five

BREAKING THE CHAINS OF BONDAGE

Why do we live in bondage, and what is it that keeps us living in bondage? It's all the things and ideas that we center our lives around and the unwillingness to change the way we think. If you are living in bondage and making excuses for not living the way God has instructed, it's time to change your thought process. As I stated in the last chapter, the mind is the seat of the soul. When we surround ourselves with negativity, the thoughts and actions are transferred to us. The negativity pierces the heart and implants evil that stems from the negativity into our soul. Once the thoughts have been embedded in the soul the spirit becomes tainted. We then governed our life based on what's implanted in us. If we change our thoughts the heart and spiritual realm will be changed.

"And be not conformed to this world;
but be ye transformed by the renewing
of your mind, that ye may prove what
is good, and acceptable, and perfect,
will of God."

Romans 12:2

Studies of the thought process revealed that it is the mind that controls us. Psychologists say that there are two mental laws. These laws contribute greatly to our state of being. One is known as the law of concentration, and the second the law of substitution. The law of concentration states that whatever we think about on a continuous basis becomes a part of us. In other words we become what we think. When we get an idea fixed in our mind, we constantly think about it and the idea become a part of us. Our mind is where the seeds are planted and they grow into either good or bad fruit. The choice of the fruit we produce is up to the individual. On the other hand, the law of substitution states that our mind can only hold one thought at a time. The mind does not care what we chose to think. Substitution states that the mind can only hold one thought whether it is positive thoughts or negative thoughts. Just as God's Word tells us we cannot live in sin and live for Him. One must choose to live for Him or a life walking in darkness. The fact is that we can control our mind. A person walks in un-forgiveness will only have a change in mind if he or she chooses to. Striving for perfection means changing our thoughts; changes in thoughts bring about a change of the heart.

> *"For as he thinketh in his heart, so is he: Eat and drink, saith he to thee; but his heart is not with thee."*
>
> Proverbs 23:7

When the mind is transformed and all things are new we will have peace.

> *"Thou wilt keep him in perfect peace, whose mind is stayed on thee: because he trusteth in thee."*
>
> Isaiah 26:3

Man is wonderfully made in the image of God, by a perfect God. Our ability to function in the world comes through our mind, will and emotions. The mind is as a gatekeeper, it decides what thoughts will be allowed in. This is the place that controls entrance into your inner being.

The heart is the center of the inner life and the source of all the forces and functions of the spirit, soul and body. Out of the heart operates actions, habits, thoughts, emotions, motives and attitudes. When a person lives in bondage, it is the motives that contribute to how a person acts in any given situation. On the other hand, one's attitude is the reason why he or she reacts the way they do. We are what we think, our thoughts are what we allow to get pass the gatekeeper of our soul. In order to strive for perfection, we must always think as a spiritual man not the carnal man.

> *"For I know the thoughts that I think toward you, saith the Lord, thoughts of peace, and not of evil, to give you an expected end."*
>
> Jeremiah 29:11

> *"And thou, Solomon my son, know thou the God of thy father, and serve him with a perfect heart and with a willing mind: for the Lord searcheth all hearts, and understandeth all imaginations of the thoughts: if thou seek him, he will be found of thee; but it thou forsake him, he will cast thee off forever."*
>
> I Chronicles 28:9

We must think thoughts of righteous living, if we are to break the chains of bondage and live a wholesome life with no missing pieces.

*"O Lord God of Abraham, Isaac, and
of Israel, our fathers, keep this forever
in the imagination of the thoughts of
the heart of thy people, and prepare
their heart unto thee."*

I Chronicles 29:18

*"The thoughts of the righteous are
right: but the counsels of the wicked
are deceit"*

Proverbs 12:5

Everything of value in a Christian's life
must flow from revelation of God into their in-
tuition and is controlled by the spirit within. The
spirit is the God conscious part of you, created
within you by God, in order to assist in striving
for perfection. The inner voice can and will urge
you to do or act in a way that is not Godly, but
the spirit reasons it out and directs you back to
God. The spirit also gives us the ability to discern
between right and wrong, and it is our source of
peace in a storm. Let's look back: the mind is the
entrance point; the heart is where the thoughts
are processed; the soul is what must be saved;
and the spirit is the driving force that instills in
us the desire to do right. The mind attracts either
good or bad thoughts. If we were to look closely
at the law of substitution, it is revealed that the
mind will draw the Word of God, or the evils of
this world. In order to fulfill God's purpose for
your life you must substitute negative thoughts

with positive thoughts, and arm yourself with the Word of God. To arm yourself means that you are ready to use God's Word when you go into battle against the corruption of the world and the desires of the flesh.

I am often approached by believers who have allowed the mind to control them and have fallen back into a life of destruction. The one thing they all have in common is a familiar statement. "I try hard to do right but every time when I am trying to do right someone makes me do wrong." I have tried hard to reason as to why we blame others for our shortcomings, and why we blame others for what's wrong in our life. The abusive husband blames his drinking problem on the issues he has to deal with at home. The husband who does not want to grow up, so he plays while the responsibilities of his household falls by the wayside. He blames the way he was brought up on the way he handles his responsibilities. The son or daughter who disrespects their parents and blames their actions on the way they were treated as a child. The Word of God tells us to honor our parents, God did not use the word "if" in this statement or "maybe." He said honor our parents. Disrespecting our parents is a sin no matter what you feel. That drug addict who places the blame on friends for the continued use of drugs. What the addict fails to realize is that he or she are the ones who controls what is put into their body. And there's that person who lies to gain control of others, and lives in a world based on lies. The chains must be broken; it's time to take the blame for our own action. Every individual is responsibility for what goes into their mind. If hatred, un-forgiveness, addictions and lust have taken root in your soul, it's because you, as the gatekeeper of your mind has open the door for the junk to come in. It's time to break the chain that binds us in foolishness and walk only in God's Word. A person must first want to be free before he or she can be freed. This can only be done by developing a close relationship with God.

> *"I the Lord have called thee in righteousness, and will hold thine hand, and will keep thee, and give thee for a covenant of the people, for a light of the Gentiles; to open the blind eyes, to bring out the prisoners from the prison, and them that sit in darkness our of the prison house."*
>
> Isaiah 42:6-7

When a person's mind is defiled and corrupted, he or she is doing nothing more than serving time in prison, self-imprisonment. If you are living in self-imprisonment you have the ability through Jesus Christ to set yourself free. Yes, you know within yourself you are not the person you should be. You are proclaiming Christianity but you are being held in bondage, still sinning, it's time to change. Stop dwelling on the negative thoughts and replace them with positive thoughts.

The addict cannot stop using if the mind is always thinking of ways to get drugs. The alcoholic cannot change if he or she is always hanging out at a bar. That lusting person cannot change if they are sitting hour after hour watching porn on television. The person who lives in the past cannot begin living in the present until he or she stops living in the past. And the person with a lying tongue cannot live in truth if he or she never speaks the truth. One living in un-forgiveness will never be able to forgive if he or she is always bringing up the wrong that was done to them. One can never know love if he or she bases all relationships on that one bad relationship. A change of mind and thoughts is the key to freedom. The choice is an individual decision. Ask yourself, will you use your mind as a conductor of the things of God or a life of corruption.

I am sure that many can relate to this example. My husband woke up one morning fourteen years ago and decided not to smoke anymore after twenty years of smoking. When he said to me, "I am not going to smoke again," my first thought was, I'll give him two hours before he starts again. I am happy to say that I was wrong, he has never smoked again. Now, you may be saying, everyone can't do that. You are right, because it takes more than simply expressing your intentions with your mouth. It takes a change in mind and a strong will to stand on what you have decided. What he did was reasoned with his mind and placed the desire in his heart, then the mind and heart came to an agreement; it was then implanted in his soul. When the mind would try to back out on the deal and try to talk him into smoking just one more, the heart would say that's not what we agreed on, the heart then reached down into the soul for backup and forced the doubting spirits out of the mind. When the heart and soul comes together and decide to strive for perfection, they do not allow the mind to continue to open the door to let junk flow through.

In Romans, even Paul wrestled with the flesh and the mindset of God. He lets us know that it hard living a spirit-filled life, the struggles are great but it can be done.

> *"For we know that the law is spiritual: but I am carnal, sold under sin. For that which I do I allow not; for what I would, that do I do not; but what I hate, that do I."*
>
> Romans 7:14-15

Paul shares with us that even he struggled with doing right. But when he had the desire to do wrong he stood strong. He understood that Jesus Christ was his way of escape just as He is ours.

> *"O wretched man that I am! Who*
> *shall deliver me from the body of*
> *death? I thank God through Jesus*
> *Christ our Lord. So then with the mind*
> *I myself serve the law of God; but with*
> *the flesh the law is sin."*
>
> Romans 7:24-25

If you are struggling with the person you are; and you know God is not happy with whom you are; you need to change the way you think. It's time to start thinking about what's right in your life, what's good instead of bad, happy times instead of the sad times. Happiness will only come when you stop crying over the problems in our lives and start thanking God for the problems we don't have. God wants to take our hand and lead us as we walk with Him. It is only when you place your hand in His, that you are in tune with Him, and can then walk in His perfect will. You can hold the thought of Christ in your mind, heart and soul, all you have to do is make the decision.

> *"For who hath known the mind of the*
> *Lord, that he may instruct him? But*
> *we have the mind of Christ."*
>
> I Corinthians 2:16

We live in an age of technology, most households own computers. Anyone who uses a computer can relate to receiving messages through e-mail. The e-mails are a way of instant communication. We also receive what we know as junk e-mail that is sometimes very annoying. The number of junk e-mail received in one day can sometimes be overwhelming. That's when you want to make sure your spam protection is working. If it is not working the way you feel it should, you start searching for upgrades to stop the junk mail from coming in. Likewise with our mind, the flesh fights to take control of the mind, always sending messages which contain impure thoughts. The flesh has a very strong desire to get in and take control of the mind because of the surroundings it has been exposed to. Satan makes sure that your mind is constantly receiving junk e-mail from the world by way of television, telephones, places of entertainment and, yes, even in the home. He works hard at making sure the mind is redirected from pure thoughts to impure thoughts. That's when one needs to check their spam protector, double-checking to make sure they are prayed up, studied up and walking in faith with a renewed mind.

> *"For if ye live after the flesh, ye shall die; but if ye through the Spirit do mortify the deeds of the body, ye shall live. For many are led by the Spirit of God, they are the sons of God."*
> Romans 8:13-14

When your mind, heart and soul are focused on Jesus, the junk e-mail doesn't stand a chance.

"Finally, brethren, whatsoever things are true, whatsoever things are honest, whatsoever things are just, whatsoever things are pure, whatsoever things are lovely, whatsoever things are of good report; if there be any good virtue and if there be any praise, think on these things.

Philippians 4:8

Earlier, I stated that being chained in bondage means that you are under the control of someone or something. It's not good to be held in bondage by the evils of this world, but there is one type of bondage in which we all need to be held captive. We all need to be wrapped up, chained from the top of our head to the bottom of our feet. We need to be bound so tightly that we are never free or never want to be freed. In this bondage, it's a wonderful thing to be controlled by the one who is holding us captive. How wonderful it is to be held in bondage by our Lord and Savior Jesus Christ. Act 12:6-9 gives us an account of being chained in the bondage of Jesus Christ.

"And when Herod would have brought him forth, the same night Peter was sleeping between two soldiers, bound with two chains; and the keepers before the door kept the prison. And, behold, the angel of the Lord came upon him, and a light shinned in the prison, and he smote Peter on the side, and raised him up, saying, Arise up quickly, and his chains fell off from his hands. And the angel said unto him, Gird thyself, and bind on thy sandals. And so he did. And he saith unto him Cast thy garment about thee, and follow me. And he went out, and followed him; and wish not that it was true which was done by the angel; but thought he saw a vision."

Acts 12:6-9

It is good to know that there is something that can break the chains that binds us. It is the Love of God that can and will break the chains that binds us through Jesus Christ. After the resurrection of Christ, He met with His disciples in the upper room for the last time before He ascended into Heaven. Jesus' message to the disciples was a declaration of peace. It was during this time that He commissioned the disciples to carry on His Work. They were to carry on the Work which He took so much time teaching them to do. Because Jesus would no longer be in their mist, they must carry on in faith. John 20:21: "Then said Jesus to them again, Peace be unto you as my Father hath sent me, even so send I you." After He said this, the Word of God tells us that Christ then breathed on them and said, "Receive ye the Holy Spirit." It was then Christ breathed His Life into the disciples, that He gave them the great responsibility of carrying on His Work through His teachings and by the guidance of the Holy Spirit.

In Acts 12:6-9 we see the apostle Peter, determined to do what he had been commissioned by God to do. The book of Acts depicts the many acts of the disciples, in other words, it shows us the disciples in action. They were active men, in action for their Heavenly Father. They laid the foundation for Christian church. They preached the Word of God. The disciples were strong men of God, held in the bondage of Jesus Christ. Carrying on the work of Jesus was not an easy task. The disciples suffered greatly as they labored for the Master. They could have turned away from God at any time but they had a made up mind, with faithfulness embedded in their heart and soul, determine to stay on the battlefield for God. The suffering was a voluntary action on the part of the disciples. They stood steadfast, being obedient servants. They were all about their Master's business. As Christians, we are Disciples of Christ, we are commissioned to carry on the Work of Jesus, we are to stand for righteousness sake and always walk in his light. When we are bound in the chains of sin, we cannot do the Will of our Father.

Because of the determination of the disciples to continue the work of Jesus the disciples were often tested. They were often caught in bad situations, by no doings of their own, only because they were doing what they were commissioned to do. The disciples stood with the mindset of striving for perfection by doing the will of God. In Acts 12, we note that Herod the King was on the warpath against Christianity. The first verse in the chapter tells us the Herod stretched forth his hands to vex the church. The word vex mean to subject to or affect with pain and suffering. Until that moment, the king could not justify taking any actions against the church, but now he had a reason. He first attacked the church through certain members of the church; this action did not stop the building of God's kingdom. So then he took a sword and killed James, the brother of John. This action made the Jews happy so Herod proceeded to take Peter as a prisoner. James was murdered and Peter was imprisoned for having a mindset to do what was right. Here you can see Satan at work. Herod was operating on behalf of Satan. When Satan set out to attack us, he starts by trying to get to us indirectly. If he is unsuccessful at these attempts, he then goes after the heart of the matter. Satan will try to conquer you anyway he can. Sometimes, he starts attacking us through our sisters and brothers, if you can endure the accusations, lying and backbiting, he then takes it to another level. He then moves to the matters of our heart and try attacking us through our spouse or children. If we continue to stand through the hurt, disappointments, misunderstandings and mental abuse, he finds another angle to attack from. Satan goes through all this trouble because he wants to bind us in a life of unbelief, a life of mistrust and corruption. He wants to bind us in a hopeless life, a life that will keep us walking in darkness, far away from the light of the Holy Word.

The king, just at Satan, did everything within his power to destroy the church. But God kept on delivering his children out of bondage over and over. Now that the king had thrown Peter in prison, he remembered that he had thrown Peter in jail before. Peter escaped so Herod took special precautions this time. He wanted to make sure that Peter would not escape again, so he assigned twelve soldiers to guard Peter around the clock, four guards at a time. Two of the guards were actually chained to Peter, which meant that every move Peter made, they too made. Peter was bounded and chained in prison, but his expectant faith and his immovable conviction allowed him to have peace in the midst of a bad situation. The peace of God is so amazing that Peter could sleep while he was physically chained to two guards. He slept with the assurance of knowing, through

Jesus Christ, he would be delivered out of this situation. In times of trouble we become restless, we allow Satan to bind us in the chains of confusion, disappointment, anger and hatred. When he binds us he knows that we are weak and have no faith.

When situations arise in your life, don't allow Satan to bind you, stand on the promises of God, stand expecting God to deliver you, stand with that immovable conviction that Peter stood on.

You might say that sometimes it's hard to stand in the time of a storm or the storms gets so rough you can't stand. But if you love God you will stand in His name no matter how much pain you have to bear. Stand knowing that God promised never to leave us or forsake us in our times of trouble.

Herod had planned to humiliate Peter in front of the people of the land. Yes, Herod had a plan but God also had a plan. Peter could sleep while he was in prison chained to the guards because he know that because he was living in the Will of God, striving for perfection, God would take care of the situation. God was busy working it out while he slept. We must have the same faith Peter had, faith which expects God to do what He promises. Faith knowing God is a God of truth. Faith that reminds us that the God we serve is a God that's never too busy to come see about us. There is assurance in knowing God never sleeps, and it is faith that prompts us to call on Him in our time of need.

Now, while Peter was in prison chained to the guards there was something else happening. One of the members of the church heard about what had happen to James, and now Peter was in prison. She knew they had lost one leader but there was still time to save the second leader. Sister Mary called a prayer meeting at her house. Peter was bounded, asleep in prison, and Mary, along with other members of the church, was praying. Don't you know there is power in prayer, especially when they are prayers of the righteous? They prayed with that expectant faith, they prayed with hope in their hearts, they prayed in faith. When I think of how Mary prayed, I think about some of the old sisters of the church today. They get some disturbing news so they call the old sisters up. I can just hear them, "Sisters, we need to pray." Prayer does change things, and God does answer prayers. I know because God heard the prayers coming from Sister Mary's house. While they were still praying, God answered their prayers. God sent an angel to loose Peter. The angel didn't go in the prison making a lot of noise, creating a disturbance, the angel just simply touched Peter in the side and the chains fell off, and he walked out of prison. Striving for perfection means there has to be much prayer time. The Christians today need to bind together and have a prayer meeting, a prayer meeting where God's people are praying without ceasing. Praying until the chain that binds our children is broken, the chains that bind our brother and sisters are broken.

We can break the chains of bondage and live in peace but we can't do it alone. It's time for us to break the chains of bondage and live a free life bound in Christ. Remember, we can't do anything by ourselves, we must do as the song writer said, "Hold to God's unchanging hand."

The angel further instructed Peter to put on his shoes and his garment, and follow him to safety. Jesus is saying to us today that we don't have to live our life bound and chained in sin, He want us to be free. Just as the angel told Peter to get dressed, we too must get dressed. Striving for perfection means you will attacked from all angles so be must be ready to fight. Our survival depends on us putting on the whole armor of God.

Break the chains of bondage that chain you to this world and chain yourself to Jesus Christ. THE CHAINS CAN ONLY BE BROKEN BY THE CHANGING OF THE MIND, BY WAY OF PRAYING, STUDYING AND MEDITATION.

Chapter Six

IT'S ALL ABOUT LOVE

In the 1980s, the singer Tina Turner recorded a song that topped the charts entitled, "What's Love got to do with it?" I've got to tell you, love has everything to do with everything in our life as well as the quality of life we live. We need to know that love is not an impersonal force, a choice, a concept or idea. But, love is a nature, an essence and a quality of being. The human reasoning of the concept of love is fragmented, distorted and unreliable and is based on feelings and emotions. The flesh tells us that love is what makes you feel good. A young lady believes because her male friend buys her fine gifts, and has the right touch he loves her. Never mind the fact that when she says the wrong thing or does something he does not like he abuses her. A few hours later when he apologizes and brings her a gift, she's sure it's because he loves her. The cycle goes on and on until someone is hurt either physically or mentally, and it's too late to see this as a distorted concept of love.

"What's love got to do with it?" Everything, because God is Love and we must understand that He is what love is all about. God is infinite, and because He is infinite the Bible does not define love, but describes love through the characteristics of God. His character is shown through what He did for us.

> *"For God so loved the world that he gave His only begotten Son, that whosoever believeth in him should not perish, but have everlasting life."*
>
> John 3:16

We must understand that love is an action word it must be expressed through actions. Love is not giving someone gifts because love is not an object, love is not something that is understood, but it is an expression through actions. When we hurt God by being disobedient, his hurt is redeemed when someone else obeys. There is action in everything God does for us, according to John 3:16 he gave, Romans 5:8 he did, and I John 4:10 he sent. Are your actions love in motion or are you just going through the motions not really connecting the word love with what you do? The greatest demonstration of love is the cross:

"Hereby perceive we the love of God, because he laid down his life for us: and we ought to lay down our lives for the brethren."

I John 3:16

When Jesus died on the cross to save us, His love was in motion; He personally took on the sins of the world. Placed them on His back carried them up Calvary's hill. Put them on the cross and died for every person that dwelled on this earth, as well as generations to come. We as sinners do not initiate our love for Him. We only reciprocate His love back to Him because He loved us first.

"We love Him, because He first loved us."

I John 4:19

The cross is personal, intense and compelling. Everyone has a need to love and be loved which can only be satisfied by what Jesus did on Calvary.

When the missing piece is love, it starves a person. Being hungry for love makes us look for love in all the wrong places. No love: the reason for running here and there, seeking love in material wealth, abusive relationships, and worshipping false gods, these things only satisfies the flesh for a short time. When the money runs out, and your body is worn from that abusive relationship and you find that those false gods are doing nothing to save you, where do you turn? Do you return to God who loved you first or do you turn to the love you initiate? One can always return to the God who loved us first by way of studying, meditating and praying. God's Love is what develops and strengthen us as we mature into what He wants us to be. He never allows us to go through more than we can handle. It is Him who equips us with what we need for every problem we encounter.

When the missing piece is love, you don't have a problem mistreating your brothers and sisters, you don't have a problem with disrespecting your parents, and you don't mind stepping over people while climbing the ladder of success. When the missing piece is love, you don't have a problem lying to cover up your wrong doings. When love is missing, you don't have a problem not out reacting to those in need. No love causes you to react after everything is over with the words, "I could have," or "would have." Some hold back on reactions until it is too late then they use the phase, "I should have." If you walk in God's Love the expressions could have, would have and should have are not words you use, instead you put your love into actions and do what has to be done without giving a second thought. After all, God did not say I could have sent my Son to die, or I would have sent my Son, or I should have sent my Son. God saw the world needed a savior and sent His Son to die for our sins. It's time to stop making excuses and blaming other for what we don't do. The time is now to put in place the missing piece of love, and when this piece is in place, your whole life will be changed.

Everyone needs to be loved. A lack of love caused them to hunger for love, which increases the fleshly need to obtain love from somewhere. The need for love causes people to seek love in others who are dealing with the same hunger. Because neither knows what real love is, they create a distorted love relationship with the end results being imperfect love. There is only one perfect love; this love comes through God the Father. He is the only one who can satisfy the craving of life within us. How we enter into a relationship determines the end results. Too many people spend time looking for love with an empty desire deep inside using the wrong approach to fine love. Because love is an action word we must enter into relationship with a plan of action. We have got to learn to approach love with the spirit of giving instead of the desire to use someone. When "self" is the focus, failure is the results. God's Word tell us that in order to be His disciple we must "deny ourselves," denying ourselves means putting aside our wants and follow God, who is Love.

We don't know how to love because so many are afraid to love because they are not in touch with their inner spirit. One day I was watching television, the commercials really got my attention. Many people were talking about love; they associated the word with things. Things can't love you, over time they deteriorate. First Corinthians the thirteenth chapter tells us what love is and is not.

> *"But the fruit of the Spirit is love, joy, peace, longsuffering, gentleness, goodness, faith, meekness, temperance: against such there is no law."*
>
> Gal. 5:22-23

The word "fruit" in the above scripture is translated as "karpos" which means growth. The scripture is saying, "But the growth of the Spirit," when you walk in the light of Jesus there is a growth, as we grow we understand how to love.

Back to the question, "what's love got to do with it?" Everything, because everything God requires of us is all about love. I took a class entitled, "The Theology of Love," the instructor taught this class with such conviction. He shared with the class a revelation God gave him while preparing for this class. He stated that the nine fruits of the spirit are distinct from the others, but the one thing they all have in common is love. Love is the motivational fruit that stimulates the others.

THE GROWTH OF THE SPIRIT IS LOVE . . .
Love is the growth of the Spirit in our lives because . . .
Joy is the expression of love,
Peace is the realization of love,
Longsuffering is the endurance of love,
Gentleness is the administration of love,
Goodness is the character of love,
Faith is the response of love,
Meekness is the disposition of love,
Temperance is the control of love.

What Love is:

LOVE IS PATIENT.
Love stays the same under pressure,
Love is constant. Impatience is a
spirit of unloved from the suffering of
inconvenience.

Love does not allow anyone to mistreat anyone just because they are stressed out or things are not going right for them. "Love is patient" means to love that child no matter how different they may be. Love is patient means saying a kind word even if the food your wife has cooked is not an eatable meal. Love is patient allows us to realize that although doing something for someone may be an inconvenience for you, you do it anyway.

LOVE IS KIND.

Love goes out of its way to be gracious, Love is gentle. Harshness is an inappropriate escape from the suffering of constraint. Love looks for a way to be constructive.

"Love is kind" does not allow you to correct someone in a belittling manner. Love is kind means your corrections are done with a sensitive heart and a soft spoken voice. Love is kind means you take a moment to tell someone just how much you appreciate them.

Love is kind means you always say please and thank you. Love is kind means you taking time to help someone who are in a bad situation. Love is kind means not acting according to your emotions but your actions are based on the need of others.

LOVE IS NOT JEALOUS

Love never overflows with jealousy. Love is always ready to rejoice when someone else receives a blessing. Love does not mean you have to impress, it means being you. Love is not envious of what someone else has.

Love is not jealous; love does not allow you to get upset because someone has been blessed with a new car and it's the one you wanted. Love is not jealous does not allow you to always find fault in everything someone else does just because you are not the one doing it. Love is not jealous, does not allow you to stop speaking to a friend because he or she received a promotion on the job. Love is not jealous, does not allow you to stop speaking to someone because they were recognized for their hard work.

LOVE DOES NOT BRAG
Boasting in self is not a part of love.
Love is not a parade where you toot
your own horn and pat yourself on the
back.

Boasting is a selfish act, when you walk in Christ you realize that life is not about you. Love does not brag on the things you have or the accomplishment you have made. It does not brag on what you can do or how much influence you think you have. Love does not brag, means biting your tongue and realizing that you are not the only one that has been blessed by God.

LOVE IS NOT ARROGANT
Love does not speak with an attitude
of looking down on others. Love is not
arrogant which means you are ap-
proachable at all times. Love is not

*conceited, does not put on fronts, does
not pump up ones' head with selfish
thoughts, Love is not filled with fleshly
pride.*

Love is not arrogant does not allow you to
walk around as if you are better than anyone
else. Love is not arrogant does not allow you
to not speak to someone because they cannot
dress like you. Love is not arrogant does not allow you to overlook that hungry homeless person. Love is not arrogant does not allow you
to respond negative when someone gives you
something. It may not be what you want but it
may surely meet a need.

LOVE DOES NOT ACT UNBECOMINGLY
*Love is not being inconsiderate, rude
or unmannerly to others. Love does
not interrupt conversations with selfish comments, slam doors or slam
down the telephone. Love is not a
raised voice. Love is a soft tone even in
reproof.*

Love does not act unbecomingly even in
a heated discussion. Love is maintaining a soft
tone even in a disagreement. Love is not yelling and screaming because things are not going
your way. Love is listening with an open mind
and searching for a solution. Love is taking the
time to see things as they really are and not

how you perceive them. Love is not jumping up and down, yelling because you can't find the remote to the television. Love allows you to know when to step away from what could be a bad situation.

LOVE DOES NOT SEEK ITS OWN
Love is not selfish. Love is not being so absorbed in oneself that you forget about others. Love is not getting for oneself but giving to others. Love is putting the needs and the desires of your family above you own needs and desires.

Love does not say to a son or daughter I'm buying myself a new car so I won't be able to send you to college. Love does not say to your wife you can't have that dress you need because I want a new fishing rod. Love is being willing to say I don't need a new fishing rod. I can use the one I have so my wife can have that new dress. Love is turning down that new hat so that your husband can pay a bill. Love is not about you, but what you can do for others. Love is stopping on the street to give that homeless person money for food.

LOVE IS NOT PROVOKED
Provoking is becoming angry enough with another person that causes one to fall out of love and into self. Love

*does not allow us to push others to
the point where they form an opinion
based on one person's action about
everyone. Causing them to look only at
the negative side of things and trusting
only in self.*

Love does not provoke does not allow that
abusive parent to mistreat a child forcing them
into a life of mistrust, and feeling unloved.
When a child is provoked they develop into a
provoked adult who unleashes his or her wrath
on society.

LOVE KEEPS NO RECORD OF WRONGS
*Love does not allow you to remember
the wrong that has been done to you.
Love does not write down things to
use against others. Love does not hurt
others with the recalling of past situations. Love does not remind anyone
of old habits when they have repented.
Love does not remember old stuff.*

Love keeps no records means that you
should never use the words, "I remember when.
Love does not remind that unfaithful husband
or wife of the past after you have forgiven them.
Love doesn't leave room in the back of your
mind for recording past events that you didn't
understand. Love does not hold your brothers
and sisters captive in sin because you choose

to keep bringing up the past; the sin is keeping the record. Love is constantly wiping the slate clean, erasing the memory and starting over in the name of Jesus. Love does not constantly remind that child of a foolish decision they made in the past.

LOVE DOES NOT REJOICE IN UNRIGHTEOUSNESS

Love does not laugh at worldly, off color jokes. Love does not find joy in wrongdoings. Love dismisses the carnal pleasures and takes on the spiritual joy. Love does not enjoy foolish jesting.

Love does not laugh when a joke is received through e-mail that belittles people.

Love does not find joy in sexually abusing someone in the name of fun. Love does not enjoy causing grief to someone based on a joke. Love is not inappropriate use of words or actions no matter what the situation may be. No, love is not giving someone the finger because they cut you off in traffic. Love is not correcting your children by using harsh words that belittles them.

LOVE BEARS ALL THINGS

When you walk in love there is never a burden too heavy to bear. Love is not easily released even when the burdens

*of the heart are heavy. True love can
get you through anything.*

It's because of love that we are able to keep
on loving, keep on giving, and keep on praying
doing a time when we feel our burdens are too
heavy to bear. It is love that makes those burdens seem lighter.

LOVE ENDURES ALL THINGS
*Love never gives up on anyone, it
stands in all situations. Love knows
no limit, and will outlast any and all
things. Love does not know how to
give up.*

Love endures when times are hard and you
feel as if you don't have a reason to live. Love
endures when a husband doesn't seem to know
where home is. Love endures with the wife who
chooses the street over staying home with her
children. It is the love of God that turns the situations we believe to be impossible in to positive endings.

The word love is not listed in I Corinthians
12:8-10 as one of the nine gifts. Therefore we
can conclude that the reason it is not mention
as a gift is because love is not a gift. Love is a
walk (Eph. 5:1-2); Love is a fruit (Gal. 5:22-23);
Love is a way (I Cor. 12:31); Love is a lesson (I
Th. 4:9) and Love is a commandment (John
15:12). Because love is a walk we must pursue

love. Because love is a fruit it must be cultivated to grow. Because love is a way we must follow in the footsteps of love. Because love is a lesson we must study love so that we can purse it, cultivate it and follow it. First and foremost, because love is a commandment it must be obeyed. It is impossible to pursue, cultivated, follow, or study if we do not obey the commandments of God.

In essences love is expressed through suffering, Jesus lived on this earth and suffered greatly not only on the cross, but on His way to the cross. Love is expressed through sacrifice.

God made the greatest sacrifice when He sent His only Son to die for our sins. A mother is who loves her children suffers in love; when she sacrifices her own needs for the needs of her children. When you love someone you suffer over their sins, their sorrows and sickness. If you have the heart of Jesus, you have a bleeding heart that overflows with compassion for everyone.

When we suffer in love we eventually become emotionally drained, but when we rejoice in love the soul is replenished. Love rejoices with the truth and is always glad when the truth prevails. Love never compromises the truth when it suffers or covers, but it speaks the truth in love. Love produces the joy of righteousness. Love believes all things and is eager to believe the best about everyone and there is no end to its trust. Love hopes all things, it is optimistic when faced with negative circumstances believing that all things work together for the good of those who love the Lord. Love keeps looking for a way to win and always find joy in loss, as well as success.

In order to love others, love must first be given to us, and it must be received. We receive love when we come to know the "Lover," God the Father. To know God is to know love. A man that does not know God does not know love. All can know love, but you must be born again. It is then that the love you will come to know is higher and more intense than a parent's love for a child. When we become filled with the Holy Spirit the love of God and understanding His power is the greatest experience one can ever have.

We as Christians must learn to spread love everywhere we go. There are so many people in the world just longing to be shown love and kindness. They are like dry kindling ready to ignite when love is expressed to them. We need to express love and dispense love as we practice the love method given to us by God through His Son Jesus Christ. Always remember that in God there is no failure, since God is Love there is no failure in love. We must reach out to others, it's that one love filled deed that can and will change a harden heart to a spirit filled heart.

If you have a desire to be free and want to fill the missing piece of love, pray and ask God to implant within you the Spirit of Love. The time is now for us to stage a war against Satan by using the weapon of love, so that others may come to know the God of Love for themselves.

Chapter Seven

STRIVING FOR PERFECTION

Striving for perfection can be compared to running an obstacle course. When one takes on the challenge of running an obstacle course it requires much dedication and endurance. Running an obstacle course requires a lot from the person taking on the task. He or she must stay focus on what he is doing because they never know what to expect. An obstacle course is filled with the unexpected and the runner is expected to stay on the course and complete it no matter how hard the course becomes. The runner must first be in physical condition able to endure and stand the test. The arms must be strong in the event he or she has to pull themselves up, the legs must be ready to move through the course from the beginning to the end. And it is very important that he or she are in good mental shape, an alert mind always thinking ahead to avoid accidents. In order to be successful on the obstacle course one must go through a time of preparation. The amount of time put into the preparation determines the outcome. The runner who spends a lot of time preparing for the course is more likely to be successful at attaining his or her goal. This too can be applied as one strives for perfection. The preparation stages must start with a willingness to change your mind and thoughts, then put in place the plan to change the way you think. Once the mind is made up, you must establish a relationship with Jesus Christ. Once in the race you must have the determination to run the race until you reach the finish line, having a made up mind not to let nothing or no one stop you.

Striving for perfection mean laying out the pieces, then they can be placed in the right spot. There must be a change in the way you think, negative thoughts replaced with positive thoughts. Changing your thoughts will change you.

"And be not conformed to this world; but be ye transformed by the renewing of your mind, that ye may prove what is that good, and acceptable, and perfect; Will of God."

Romans 12:2

No one really like changes, but God continually calls for changes in our life. If you don't want to change, there is no reason to even think about striving for perfection. Without change there is no growth, changing your thoughts from the world to the Word of God will ensure spiritual growth.

> *"That ye put off concerning the former conversation the old man, which is corrupt according to the deceitful lusts; And be renewed in the spirit of your mind; and that ye put on the new man, which after God is created in righteousness and true holiness."*
>
> Ephesians 4:22-24

Society leads us to believe that we can change what is considered a sin. There are many things that changes in our lives. Friends come and go, financial status may change, our family members may walk away, and our health change. But God's Word still remains the same. We must understand that what God labeled as a sin will forever be a sin, His Word never changes.

> *"Jesus Christ the same yesterday, and today and forever."*
>
> Hebrews 13:8

The changes for good have to start within you. Changing the way you think, the things you do and your reactions. Sometimes we have to change the people we associate with. We may have to distant ourselves from family members. It's time to stand in the mirror and take a long hard look at ourselves. But make sure your turn on the light first, because it's impossible to see the real you in the dark. Ask yourself as to whether or not you are ready for a change, do you desire a change. If when looking in the mirror you are dissatisfied with yourself, you are ready for a change. If you are satisfied with what you see you are not ready for a change. One must allow the Holy Spirit to convict them and it is then that the change begins.

We are human so we must know that because we are human we are both helpless and powerless therefore striving for perfection can only be accomplished by the help of God through His Son Jesus Christ. This journey is all about letting God take control of your mind, body and soul. We try to control events in our lives as well as the people in our lives, this allows us to feel secure and in control. No matter what method your use, or how hard you work at perfecting your life. If you continue to try to control your destiny you are setting yourself up to fail. Too often we try to solve problems based on the human's point of view. We cannot solve problems based on what the flesh feels. After all it was that human nature that got you into that situation in the first place. Striving for perfection means we must stop, look at the mess in our life and say I can't do this by myself, I trust you God and I need you.

"Trust in the Lord with all thine heart; and lean not unto thine own understanding. In all thy ways acknowledge him, and He shall direct thy paths."

Proverbs 3:5-6

It takes courage to stand and say I've been doing it my way a long time and it's not working, so I surrender my all to you Lord. Once you have accepted the fact that you are absolutely powerless when it comes to controlling your life, you can then turn you life over to your Creator. Turning your life over frees you from the desires and obsessions with other people, or circumstances. This freedom makes us more comfortable with our lives because a great burden has been lifted. It is so important that we turn our life over to God. And when we turn it over to Him let Him be in control of your life. Letting go is essential if you wish to bring order into your life. Letting go means you stop fighting with problems and circumstances you cannot change and get on with living life striving for perfection. When we say that we are letting go and turning it over to God we must mean it and then our life's direction will be changed. The only thing we can control is our mind, thoughts and feelings. Knowing God means our mind, thoughts, and feelings are no longer worldly thoughts, but Godly thoughts. The real power and the only power is God, and God knows how to work things out for your good. Turn it over and let Him work it out, take your hands off and you will see His Glory.

> *"I can do all things through Christ which strengthen me."*
>
> Philippians 4:13

Placing all the missing pieces in place so that we rightfully strive for perfection means humbling yourself. The word "humble" is defined as respectful, obliging, lowly, and humiliate. The definition that I am partial too is the verb humiliate. Striving for perfection means to humiliate oneself by doing things or acting in a lowly manner. When you humiliate yourself for God, man frowns upon your actions, but God smiles. To be humiliated for the glory of God is misunderstood by men, but a welcomed praise by God. When I think of humiliation, I think of King David. Every time I read about King David and the messy situations he would get into, my heart becomes filled with joy. Why is my heart filled with joy when David was constantly in and out of bad situations? My heart is filled with joy because I realize that David knew how to do what many of us have no idea on how to even begin. David knew how to humble himself before God. Talk about total submission, David humbled himself, to the point of humiliation when he danced naked before God. David danced, praising God, and in his praising he danced out of his clothes. David had no shame when it came to praising God. But his wife on the other hand could not understand David's actions. She saw it as being shameful for the king to be reacting in such a manner. David didn't let the position of king stop his from praising God; he didn't care what others thought. He knew what God had done for him and would do for him. What a wonderful display of Love. I stated earlier that love is an action word. We show God we love him by what we do for him. David loved God so much and his actions showed God how much.

King David had many characteristics. He was a warrior, a musician, a prophet, and a king. In spite of all these wonderful characteristics, he had another characteristic, one that was not a great title, he was a sinner. In David's writing, we can see his constant struggles throughout the book of Psalm. When David was described as a man after God's heart, it was not because of his sinless life, but because he knew how to humble himself before God and ask for forgiveness. I am very partial to Psalm 40.

"I waited patiently on the Lord; and
he inclined unto me, and heard by cry.
He brought me up also out of a hor-

*rible pit, out of the miry clay, and set
my feet upon a rock, and established
my goings. And he hath put a new
song in my month, even praise unto
our God' many shall see it, and fear,
and shall trust in the Lord."*

One sin that truly stained David's character was the deceitful way he plotted to gain the soldier's wife for himself. David's life was like a roller coaster, up and down. I don't know what the situation was when David wrote the 40th Psalms, but his writing revealed that he once again was entangled in sin; David was once again in a muddy mess. I say muddy mess because David said, "He pulled me out of the miry clay." Clay is made of dirt and water that formulate mud.

One living in the world of the world is just like David, a muddy mess, but just as David, you don't have to stay in the mess. God will pull you out. All you got to do is ask Him. David said, "I waited patiently, on the Lord and He inclined unto me and heard my cry." David knew it was God who would come and pull him out of his mess over and over again. He also knew that God would step in on time, that's why he said he waited patiently. David had faith and trust in God. Without faith, David would have never been able to call on God with the expectation of Him hearing his cry. Just as David, when the roller coaster of life is at the bottom of the hill we must have faith and then wait patiently on God.

Usually, when we find ourselves in a muddy mess, the mess has been creeping up on us for a long time. One sin leads to another and another until you are in a situation where you no longer know what to do. It's then that you must go to God. Pray in faith, and ask Him to clean you up. After you have prayed in faith wait on Him, after all you were patient when you were getting into that mess. So be patient knowing God will come and deliver you. Now, just because He may not come when you want Him to, don't accuse Him of forsaking you. God never leaves us or separate himself from us. We walk away from Him when we make a decision to live our lives in a clay pit.

It's not hard to tell when someone is in a muddy mess. The sinful situations bring out the worst in an individual, because sin is a separation from God. When we are separated from God the emotion of fear overtake us. Once fear has overtaken our spirit the spirit of righteousness is suppressed, we then walk in a different direction. The direction is the path of the world instead of a path of righteousness. When you find yourself in the clay pit of sin, pray for deliverance, trust in God knowing He will deliver you. God make us a promise that I stand on, He promised never to leave us or forsake us, therefore we must know God will show up and pull you out of the miry clay.

David also said, "The Lord heard my cry." This lets us know that David cried out to God. He didn't run here and there crying out to friends or family members seeking their advice. David cried out to the Lord because he remembered the times God had answered his prayers in the past. He thought about the times when God saved his life. He knew without a doubt that waiting on God would end in positive results. The Word of God tells us that God inclined unto David and heard his cry. When you decide that you no longer want to be a muddy mess, don't run to friends, running here and there trying to find answers through worldly messengers. So many times we go to people seeking guidance only to learn their life is in a bigger mess than yours. You must seek the one who can take your hand and pull you out of the miry clay.

David said, "He brought me out of the miry clay." Now, God has brought us all of us out of the miry clay a least one time. Our beginning was from dirt. The word "miry" means muddy, swampy, and slushy. Clay is a substance in the soil with the ability to retain a large amount of water. Clay makes soil thick and heavy, it contains no air so it does not allow water to evaporate, it absorbs water. The more water it absorbs the heavier the clay gets. It turns into a very heavy substance, if you try to walk through there is a great possibility of getting stuck in the clay.

I remember as a child, the streets in the community I grew up in were made of clay. The city would send tractors into the community and they would mix clay with dirt and scrap the street mixing the two together to get the bumps out of the street. Now that was fine until it rained, if there was an excessive amount of rain it was just about impossible to drive on certain streets. If you drove on them you had to be very careful to stay in the path made by other cars. If you got out of that path you would get stuck in the mud. In order to get out of the mud another car would have to pull you out. Even then it wasn't an easy task. Sometimes the car doing the pulling would get stuck also. We must be careful, when you see someone in a muddy mess, if you try to pull them out make sure you have a plan and are well equipped for the job. First, you need to know that they want to get out of the mess, because in your pulling out you too can get stuck in the mess with them. Sometimes a person may believe that they are equipped, but they are not as equipped as they believed. Some of the sins of others look good to us, especially if it involves money, and we are made to believe that we can gain from the sin. Satan's job is to pull others into the miry clay, especially if one is walking with God. On the other hand, if you are the one needing to be pulled out of the clay, be mindful of whom you seek for help. Not everyone you reach out to can help you and not everyone want to see you change. Instead of helping to pull you out they push you deeper. When you look at your life and it appears to you that you are standing in the mist of mud pit, sinking fast and there seems to be no way out. David wrote another Psalm, one that extends us an invitation to taste and see the goodness of God.

> *"I sought the Lord, and He heard me, and delivered me from my fears. They looked unto Him, and were lightened: and their faces were not ashamed. The poor man cried, and the Lord heard him, and saved him out of all his troubles. The angel of the Lord encampeth, round about them that fear him, and delivereth them. O taste and see that the Lord is good; blessed is the man that trusteth in Him."*
>
> Psalm 34:4-8

David was one who could surely extend this invitation because of the situations he often founded himself facing. Over and over again he was afforded the opportunity to taste of the wonderful love of God. David said, "I sought the Lord, and He heard me and delivered me from my fears." David put his trust in the only one who could change him, the situations in his life and the circumstances. One of the biggest downfalls of man is that we put too must trust in ourselves and others. We trust ourselves to make things right in our life rather than trusting in God. We allow fear to take control of our mind and then we try to take control of whatever is causing the fear instead of letting God handle the situation. Have you ever notice that even Christians who proclaim to have faith give in to fear. They allow the mindset to wonder and gradually become men and women living in fear and unbelief. We must stop placing conditions on trusting God and just praise Him for being God the giver of life. We need to spend more time making sure everything is well with our soul. Striving for perfection means standing on a solid foundation, are you standing on solid ground or are you standing in sinking sink.

In the 34th Psalm, David continually reminds us that God is one who answers prayers and will deliver us from all of our fears. Just take a look over your shoulder and glance back at your past. Just look at all the trials and tribulations He's brought you through. "O taste and see that the Lord is good." He was there when that husband or wife was being contrary. He was there when your children were making foolish decisions. He was there when you were walking in darkness, shielding your from all hurt, harm and danger. It was Him who turned on the light in your life so that you could see where you were going. "O taste and see that the Lord is good."

I stated that David extended us an invitation to "taste and see" but David was not the original sender of that invitation. David was saying don't take my word taste and see for yourself. At some time or another we have all received an invitation in the mail, so often we put it aside, forgetting we have received it. I asked you now to go back and check your mail because somewhere in the mist of that junk mail is an invitation. Most times we receive an invitation we are expected to bring a gift. This invitation comes with no strings attached. It is extended to us solely out of love. The only thing you have to bring to this affair is a yielding spirit, a heart of love and a mind stayed on Jesus. Yes, there are some conditions to accepting this invitation. The first condition is you must come just as you are. You don't have to run out and buy a new suit or dress. You don't have to wait until you change something in your life. He wants you to come and He will do the rest. The second condition is that He does not want your coming to be based on what everyone else is doing. He wants you to accept this invitation because you want to change and is concern only with your salvation. He does not want you to concern yourself with the reason why others are coming. Your reason for attending this great feast must be based on you and your desire to put all the missing pieces in place so that you can strive for perfection. There is another condition of accepting this invitation, you must RSVP through Jesus Christ. There are times when we receive an invitation in the mail that asks us to RSVP by a certain date. Sometimes we misplace the invitation and RSVP late, and sometimes we don't even bother to RSVP, we just go anyway. This invitation for our Heavenly Father has no deadline, you can answer anytime in your life, but whenever you decide to answer you must go through His Son Jesus Christ. Jesus is the Bread of Life that God has provided for us as food for our soul. "O taste and see."

Taste is a very important part of our human makeup. The kind of food we eat and how much food we eat depends on the taste of the food. Our taste buds are small mounds grouped together on our tongue. When food is taken into the month the taste buds transmit information about the food to the brain, if the taste is good we want more, if the taste is not so good we reject it. Once the food is placed in the mouth and the taste buds kick in, if we like the taste, we begin to chew. Chewing is the process of grinding up the food to deposit into the body. Another meaning of chewing is meditation. When one meditates on something it is a process of depositing something into the mind that affects your whole life. When we chew our food, we meditate on it absorbing the flavor and enjoying the taste. Food based on taste will either make us healthy or sick. Chewing on God's Word will make us spiritually healthy. Sometimes the taste of God's Word is bitter, but it's bittersweet. Although the taste is sometimes bitter, the end results are sweet.

Imagine yourself sitting down to a meal, one of those meals prepared by Grandma, one that has taken hours to prepare, a meal so grand that we'll call it a feast. I prefer to use the word feast in lieu of meal because usually an event where there is an abundance of food, it is considered a feast. At this feast there is something for everyone's taste. As you sit down to the table you look around at all the food, wondering where you will start. How will you taste all the food on the table without making yourself sick? You just decide to dive in, you began to eat the food enjoying every bite, trying all the different kinds of food, indulging and enjoying all the favors. You eat until you can't eat anymore. We think this is a glorious time, but there is a dark side to sitting down to such a feast. Once you have eaten the good taste is no longer in your mouth, your stomach is full but something is missing. Your soul is still hungry. After a while the feast at Grandma's house is only a memory and a few extra pounds added to the waist line.

The special invitation we received from God invites us to eat at His table. This is no ordinary table. As we sit down to this table there is a noticeable different in this table and Grandma's table. Grandma's table was filled with many different dishes. At His table the meal consists of one dish. The one dish contains the meat, vegetables and desert, all wrapped in one. It is served in the form of bread, not colonial bread, not sunbeam bread, but the Bread of Life, the Lamb of God. Now before you reach for a piece of this bread I must warn you, just one taste of this bread can and will change your whole life. Are you ready for a change in your life? I surely hope so because this bread will do something to you. One taste will change your walk, when you eat of this bread you begin your walk as if you've got on new shoes, there's a new strut in your step. The places you use to go, you feet won't carry you there anymore. It will change the way you talk, negative words become positive words. It will change your whole concept of life. A taste of this bread will clean you up, wash your sins away and make you whole. A taste of this bread will make your family and friends turn their backs on you. Tasting of this bread will bring you out of darkness into the light of God. Are you prepared to walk in His Light? Tasting of this bread will make you treat everybody right. Tasting of this bread will remove all envy, and malice from your heart, replacing it with love. Can you handle what tasting of this bread will do in your life? You must be sure that you want to taste of this bread because one taste is all it takes. If when you taste of the bread and decide to keep on eating it, God expects something. God expects you to deny yourself and live only for Him. Do you want to taste and see?

It is not unusual when gathered at a table eating with other for someone to ask another person about the taste of a certain food. If the person says it is good we try it, but if they say it's just okay we probably will leave it on the table. Just because something is good to someone else does not mean it will be good to you. You must taste of the Bread of Life for yourself, because everyone who has tasted of the Bread of Life has been touch in a different way. Your needs from the Bread of Life may not be the same as another needs. That's why you must taste and see for yourself. If you plan on getting filled with the Bread of Life you just can't rush to the table and gobble down the food. You must chew on the goodness of God, chew on His Love for you, chew on the presence of Him in your life, just chew and enjoy. After chewing for a while, you can then introduce your spirit to the Holy Spirit making the Holy Spirit a part of you. Get the taste of the Holy Spirit in your blood allow it to digest so that you will be able to reap all the benefits. The Holy Spirit will change every aspect of your life. Instead of crying in time of sorrow, you will praise God, and when misunderstandings arise, you are ready to forgive. When your friends don't understand you, it okay because you have a new friend who does understand. Instead of worrying when you are down to your last dime, you put your trust in God. "O taste and see that the Lord is good."

Many of us love bread and crave it with every meal. Bread is a starch, when bread is chewed on it begins to taste sweet. That's because starches turn to sugar, making it very appealing to the taste. Chewing on the Bread of Life can give you the same satisfaction. The more you chew on Jesus the sweeter He gets. "O taste and see."

My dad loved ice cream; he could eat it several times a day. Sometimes my mother would make homemade ice cream. The first serving would always go to my dad. I remember after he would eat his first bowl, she would ask him about the taste. She needed to know if she needed to add more sugar. He would always answer, "It is fine, it tastes like more." This was his way of asking for more ice cream. When we taste the Bread of Life our answer should be the same as his, it tastes like more. Every bite you take of the Bread of Life will taste like more. "O taste and see."

Chapter Eight

ALONE, BUT NOT ALONE

One of the main attractions of living a worldly life is always being surrounded by people who we consider to be our friends. Most often it's not what they are doing for you, but what you can do for them. It's a fact that people tend to be there for you when they have something to gain. I met a young lady who recently had decided to trade in her worldly lifestyle for a new life, walking in the Word of God. I commended her for realizing that the life she was living was one with no good end, one of self destruction. Her lifestyle involved heavy drinking and drug usage, hanging in night clubs every opportunity she had. She neglected her family for a life of what she considered fun with her friends. She went to a job everyday for the purpose of working to be able to go out and hang with her friends. And of course, she was the one with the job so she was the one bearing the expense for her friends as well. She shared with me that she would get paid on Fridays and by Sunday night she was borrowing money to make it to the next pay day.

Now keep in mind the friends that she spent her money on was not able or willing to return the favor when she was in need. Every time I had an opportunity to meet with her to discuss God's Word she would always express the need to have the approval from her friends. For some reason, she felt that she could start a new life carrying old luggage. Just because she had decided to turn her life around she believed that her friends would come on board and be part of her new direction. She would constantly express her desire to make her friends happy. I soon realized that she was missing pieces, especially the piece of trust. Even though she confessed with her mouth, and had the desire in her heart, she didn't have a change in her mindset. She maintained the mindset of pleasing others and not trusting God. Instead of building a relationship with God, she was working hard to maintain her relationship with her friends.

When the decision is made to make any type of change in your life, everyone will not be on board with you. Sometimes it's the ones you believed to be your closest friends who will be the first to walk away from you. Those who have a need to have the approval of friends are easy prey for Satan to attack. When Satan sees our weakness, he uses them for his good. It is our weakness that keeps us living in sin. In this young lady's case, she understood that her lifestyle was not a desirable one, she spoke of the desire to change but she kept looking back hoping that her friends would follow her so she would not be alone. Too often we desire to take familiar things with us when we leave for a new journey. What she did not understand is that the decision to accept our Lord and Savior is an individual decision. Just because you make the decision to turn your life over to Christ, does not mean that family and friends will get on board.

When God told Lot to take his family and leave Sodom. The instructions were not to look back, just walk away and look ahead. The pull of sin caused Lot's wife to want to take just one last look back. Because she made the decision to look back, God turned her into a pillar of salt. There's something about sin that makes you want to look back, revisit was we called the fun times, the times when the fleshly needs were being satisfied. The young lady looked back, and the fun times and the fleshy needs were victorious. She kept looking back wanting her friends to be there with her, when that didn't happen she decided to join them. She went back in a familiar place, the world, once again financing her friends' worldly lifestyle. Her failure to continue her walk with God was based on her friends. She did not want to be alone, she was afraid of traveling an unfamiliar road. She believed without her friends she would be alone.

New converts are not the only ones who allow themselves to be influenced by friends. There are those who proclaim to be Christians who also allow this to happen. In the church some formed what we call cliques. The leader of the clique is usually someone who displays a stronger personality trait than the others. This person usually dictates to the others, planting negative seeds in their spirit based on what they feel. Rather than standing alone, they allow someone to dictate where they will spend eternity. When you know what's right, you have got to take a stand. There will be no one standing in front of the judge on judgment day but you. You will be judged based on you not anyone else, or what you did because of someone else. Don't let anyone decide where you will spend eternity. Stand if you must stand alone. Once the decision is made to live in the Word of God, we must stand on His Word if we have to stand alone. You may long for family and friends to join you, but many will instead turn their back on you, but you must continue to walk in the Word. You may feel as though you are walking alone but you are not. God made a promise to each of us, He promised never to leave or forsake us.

"In the day, he which shall be upon the housetop, and his stuff in the house, let him not come down to take it away; and he that is in the field, let him likewise not return back. Remember Lot's wife. Whosoever shall seek to save his life lose it; and whosoever shall lose his life shall preserve it."

Luke 17:31-33

Now, do not misunderstand, God wants us to have relationships, because he is a God who desires a relationship with us. But, he does not want us in a relationship that will end in destruction. Desiring relationships are a nature part of our human makeup. Even Jesus on His way to the cross desired to be surrounded by friends. In the Garden of Gethsemane, Jesus took Peter, James and John to with him to the garden as he prayed to His Father. They were with Jesus, but they slept while He prayed. Although the three were with Jesus, He was alone in the burdens He had to bear. There are times when we are surrounded by friends, but we feel all alone. We all have burdens to bear. Sometimes they may seem too heavy to bear. Our friends and loved ones are there physically, but you still have this sense of loneliness deep inside of you. You may talk to friends but you still feel as if you are alone. Understand that although you may feel alone you are not alone. God is with you even when friends are not there. He is with you even with your family turn their backs on you. He is there when that husband or wife is being controlled by sin. He is there when you are dealing with disobedient children.

When you chose to walk in the light of God it sometimes gets mighty lonely on this journey, but you are not alone. If you are seeking the prize you must run this Christian race with faith.

"Wherefore, seeing we also compassed about with so great a cloud of witnesses, let us lay aside every weight, and the sin which doth so easily beset us, and let us run with patience the race that is set before us. Looking unto Jesus the author and finisher of our faith who for the joy that was set before him endured the cross, despising the same, and is set down at the right hand of the throne of God."

Hebrews 12:1-2

There are very few television shows that get my attention, but I like to watch instructional shows. Once I watched and instructional show on how to build a soapbox race car. When building a soapbox car the designer can use whatever material he desire. But in choosing the material to build this car there are some factors to consider. If the car is being built to win a race, the material must be as light as possible, without extras that would make the car too heavy. The driver's weight and size had to be considered as well. Even though the starting point of the race would be on a hill the car do not need any unnecessary weight holding it back. If the car is light and free from excess material, the possibility of winning the race is greater.

Hebrews 12:1-2 cautions us as against being loaded with unnecessary baggage. Once we began on this journey we are in a race. A race that must be ran with patience and perseverance. In this race one must have the pieces of patience and perseverance if they plan on running until the race is finished. The piece of patience is needed to help us as we encounter the difficulties that lie ahead. We need the piece of perseverance to resist all temptations that we will come up against. Another very important piece is faith, which must be out front clearing the road as we run the race. Sometimes when we sign up for the race we make the race harder than what it really is. We enter the race carrying a lot of useless baggage. If one's faith is strong, they quickly understand that they must drop the baggage it in order to run the race. On the other hand, there are those who like to hold onto what they have and run the race at the same time. Some even pick up junk to put into their bags as they run this race. If you are going to run this race until the finish line, you must lay aside every weight that will hinder you from finishing.

Satan does everything he can to overload us with excessive worldly baggage that entangles us in the cares of life causing us to lose focus on finishing the race. We must unload everything that will not contribute to finishing the race. Excess weight comes to us in one of two ways, the weight that comes to us through life's circumstances or stuff that is dumped on us by others. We cannot allow the woes of life and the junk of others to deter us from God's purpose for our lives.

I am sure we all at some time or another have felt as if the weight of the world was on your shoulder and there is no one in the world but you. You look back at all the good you have done for others. Then you think about how often the good deeds were misunderstood and considered by others to be deeds done for personal gain. You go to great length to make sure your loved ones don't have to worry. But yet, you are walked on, beat up with tongues of gossip, backbitten by those you trusted. What an awful feeling of loneliness. Then you pray to God and it seems as if He has forgotten about you. Then you remember reading in God's Word where it tells us that it okay to weep, because weeping may endure for a night, but joy comes in the morning. Faith is what will see you through such times.

It's the storms in our life that makes us stronger and more determine in our Christian walk. I travel about 20 miles a day to and from work, most of my driving on the interstate. One day in my commune home while on the interstate I ran into a very bad storm. The storm kept getting worst the further I traveled. I noticed the cars around me, there were some who pulled over. As I traveled a little further there were some who slowed down, but continued their journey. On the other hand, there were those who continued to travel at an excessive speed, with no regards to the fact that they were endangering others as well as themselves. As I watched the cars I thought about how the drivers resembled Christians in their walk with God. On this Christian journey there will be storms that come into our lives. Ask yourself, when a storm comes into my life how do you handle the storm. Are you the driver that pulls to the side of the road to wait out the storm? Then when the storm is over you get back on your journey. The problem with this solution is what happens in your life while you are waiting for the storm to past. Are you trying to handle whatever is causing the storm yourself by looking for your own solutions? Are you looking to others to correct the situation? What about God? This driver has little or no faith and can easily return to the world when a storm comes into their life.

Are you the driver that continues on the same speed as if nothing is happening? The Christian that continues on without taking any precautions do so with no regards to others. When in the storm, they work hard to come out of the storm not caring about whom they hurt or the harm they may cause to someone else. All they care about is getting through the storm even if it takes stepping on and over others. This driver is inconsiderate, selfish and lacks the piece of compassion.

And there is the driver that runs into a storm. This driver slows down but proceeds. This driver does not give up he or she stay in the storm, continues on the journey. This driver represents the Christian that is grinded and rooted in their walk. This Christian is one determine to stay on the right path no matter how bad the storm gets. They go through the storm with patience and perseverance, the patience that will help them wait out the storm and the perseverance that will not allow them to yield to temptations. This driver has faith and knows without a doubt that God will see them through the storm. This driver knows what prayer can do. Prayer will bring you through your storms. Pray without ceasing.

I am reminded of a story of a young lady that was traveling with her father. On their journey they ran into a very bad storm. She saw the cars pulling over, and asked her father should she pull over, he said no keep going.

Then she saw cars speeding around her as if it was no storm. She asked her father should she speed up, he said no keep going, don't change anything. As the storm got worst she noticed that some of the cars that had sped passed them had pulled to the side of the road. So she asked her father again, should I pull over, the storm seems to be getting worst, he said keep going. Every time she wanted to give up he kept telling her to keep going. Now she kept going because she trusted her father, and knew that she would be alright since he had taken care of her all of her life and she had trust in her father. As they continued to travel they soon ran out of the storm. The father said to his daughter, now pull over, she was a little confused, but she did as he asked. She pulled to the side of the road, he told her to look back. When she looked back she could still see the storm and the cars beside the road. She asked him, why pull over now. He said; I want you to see that because you kept going you are out of the storm, but the cars that pulled to the side of the road are still in the storm. All you needed to do was do as I asked and trust me. It was then that she realized that she shouldn't have been worried because her father was with her and he would not do anything that would hurt her. She then understood the importance of obedience.

Children of God, when you are going through the storm of sickness, stay in the storm. When you are burden down with financial obligations and can't see your way out, stay in the storm. When you receive papers declaring foreclosure from the bank, stay in the storm. When your husband or wife spends more time in the street than at home, stay in the storm. When you don't agree with your children's lifestyle, stay in the storm. When you do not get that job you applied for, stay in the storm. When you are mistreated, stay in the storm. When you try you best, but it seems as if your best is not good enough, stay in the storm. In the storms of life, you may feel alone but you are not alone. Your Heavenly Father is in the storm with you, always remember He loves you and will never allow harm to come to you. Even though you may feel as if you are alone, you are not. It's in the storms of life that He takes us in His loving arms and rocks us like babies until the storm is over. We must have the pieces of faith, hope and joy in place before the storm starts. Having these pieces in place means having faith, and hope in God through all things. And at the end of the storm He will give us joy. You may feel alone in this world, but you are not alone.

The song writer, C. Austin Miles, did a wonderful job expressing the joys of being alone with God. He expressed this through his song, entitled "In the Garden."

"I come to the garden alone, while the dew is still on the roses; And the voice I hear, falling on my ear, The Son of God discloses. He speaks in the sound of His voice. Is so sweet the birds hush their singing; And the melody that He gave to me within my heart is ringing. I'd stay in the garden with Him. Though the night around me be falling; but He bids me go—thru the voice of woe, His voice to me is calling. And He walks with me and He talks with me, And He tells me I am His own, and the joy we share as we tarry there, None other has ever known."

There are times when even through you are surrounded by family and friends you may feel as Jesus did in the garden. Alone, with the weight of the world on your shoulders, but if you have a relationship with God that you have built through Jesus Christ, you are not alone. When I am feeling alone, I find a resting place, a place of peace because I do have a relationship with Him. And I reflect on the song by C. Austin Miles. When I am lonely there is a garden I can go to, I go alone because I am going to be with a friend once I am there. I can go there anytime, but the early morning is very special. As I enter into the garden I see the beauty of God's creation. I look at the beautiful flowers then I notice how the dew is on the roses. Then I hear a voice, it is God speaking to me, such a wonderful sound.

When He speaks it's so sweet that the birds stop their sweet singing to listen. I am at such peace in the garden until I stay so long that I lose track of time, before I realize it night has fallen. When parting time comes he bids me to go on my way, but I can hear Him calling me in my heart as I leave the garden. When I think back over the time how He walked with me and talked with me all day. O, what a good time we have together, I may feel alone in this world, but I'm not because He has told me that I am His. No one could ever know the joy of being with my Lord and Savior all day long unless they come to the garden. Spending time with Him ensures that all my pieces are in place. And every time I go to the garden the pieces are bonded in place. Bonded, ensuring that the pieces of my relationship with God remain in place.

WHEN YOU WALK WITH GOD YOU ARE NEVER ALONE.

Chapter Nine

THE VITAL PIECE

When putting togeth-
er a puzzle there is something special about
putting the last piece in place. That's because
the last piece is the vital piece for completion.
When the last piece is in place, you know that
you are finally going to see the finish product
of something you have worked so hard to complete. I stated in an earlier chapter how I was
missing the last piece of the puzzle that I was
putting together. I was determine to complete
the puzzle so I got on my hands and knees and
searched everywhere for that last piece. When
I founded the piece I was one happy person, I
told everyone who would listen about finding
the last piece of the puzzle. Just as the last piece
of the puzzle represents the finish product, Jesus
Christ is the vital piece in our life that represents
completion. He should be the first and the last

piece that completes the puzzle of your lives. I say first and last because the piece that I am referring to is known as the Alpha and Omega, the beginning and the end. Do you know the vital piece?

> *"Whom do men say that I the Son of Man am? And so they said, Some say John the Baptist, some Elijah, and others Jeremiah or one of the prophets." He said to them, "But whom say ye that I am?" And Simon Peter answered and said, Thou art the Christ, the Son of the living God."*
>
> Matthew 16:13-16

At the time when Jesus asked the question in the scripture above, He knew that his time on this earth was drawing to an end. It was now time for Him to reveal and to make sure the disciples understood His deity. Surely, Jesus knew the answer when He asked this question, but His disciples needed to proclaim that Jesus is the Son of the living God. The Holy Spirit revealed to Peter who Jesus truly is, so Peter answered Jesus, "You are the Christ, the Son of the living God. The reason that Peter could answer the question was because Peter had a relationship with Jesus. He was there when Jesus performed His miracles, Peter sat under His teachings, Peter followed as Jesus lead. When you have a relationship with someone you begin to feel what they feel, you think as they think and you act as they act. Who do you say Jesus Is? Do you have a relationship with Him or are you merely acquainted with Him? Being acquainted with Jesus means you are familiar with Him because you have heard about Him. Or you know someone that has a relationship with Him and told you about Him. Because Jesus is the vital piece needed to make your life complete, you must have a relationship with Him.

Have you ever seriously asked yourself, "Who do I say Jesus Is?" Is he someone who you seek when you want to receive his gifts? Someone you call on in times of trouble? Or someone you simply hear about when you attend church? I overheard a conversation recently. One person asked the other was she still going to the gym. She said no, I just pay my money, but the other person made this comment about what she said. She said, "Going to the gym was like attending church. You have to stay in the habit of going because when you stop it's hard to go back." I thought to myself doesn't she realize the church is not just a habit? The church is in your heart. Jesus is not a habit but a way of life. As a matter of fact He is life. He is life because He is the Giver of Life.

"Who being the brightness of his glory, and the express image of his person, and upholding all things by the word of his power, when he had by

*himself purged our sins, sat down on
the right hand of the Majesty on high;
being made better than the angels,
as he hath by inheritance obtained a
more excellent name than they."*

Jesus Christ the Son of God is the vital piece, if in place He can and will free us from the chains that bind us. Hebrews the first chapter tells us that Jesus is the Son of God. The third verse tells us that Jesus is the expressed image of his Father as well as the brightness of God's glory. There are some who believe that Jesus was just an angel. But the Word of God tells us that God made him better than angels. The only one above Him is God His Father, so Jesus in no way can be compared to angels. Jesus sits at the right hand of His Father. He holds the highest position over creation. Christ represents love and righteousness this was shown to us by his obedience to his father. Jesus Christ is love and he put his love into action when he gave his life for our sins. Again I ask, who do you say Jesus Is?

Jesus Christ in an intercessor, He is always interceding with God for us. The Word of God tells us that no one can come to the Father unless they come by way of Jesus Christ. In the Old Testament, it was the priest went to God on behalf of the people. Now, because Jesus died for our sins, we can go to God ourselves. But you must believe in Jesus and what He did for us before you can go to Him. The way to God is by way of the cross that represents Jesus Christ. We try to do so many things our way but we must conform to the order of God. If we are to strive daily for perfection, it must be done through the Father, the Son and the Holy Spirit. It's time to place our trust in God and walk as our big brother, Jesus Christ. We do this by walking in love, truth and the Spirit as we develop a relationship with Him.

I've asked you on several occasions in this chapter "Who do you say Jesus Is?" As I look through the writings of the four gospel writers, Matthew, Mark, Luke and John, it became even more obvious to me who Jesus is. Who Jesus is can be seen in the many marvelous works of our Lord and Savior. Shared with us by those who spent personal time with Him and who had a personal relationship with Him. The fifth chapter of Matthews says He is a teacher, and a lawyer, He taught the disciples how to live and He showed them how to fulfill the land. Not only was He a teacher, but a preacher, His sermon on the mount gave a lot of instructions for those who desire to strive for perfection. Matthew chapter sixteen tells us that He will feed the hungry. The twentieth chapter of Matthew tells us that He gives sight to the blind. Luke chapter seven tells us that He is the forgiver of sins. Luke chapter seven also tells us that He is someone the wind and the waters obey. John chapter eleven tells us that He is a friend, and one that can raise the dead. John chapter twelve says He can predict the future, because He predicted his own death. Jesus, our big brother, walked this earth, healing the sick, raising the dead, giving sight to the blind, and saving souls. Everything He did was done out of love and obedience. We must learn to be obedient, and learn to act and not react. Jesus is our big brother, righteous living mean following the example of Jesus Christ.

Jesus, to me is my doctor in my sick room. My mediator, when I need to go to the Father. He provides when I am down to my last dollar and there are still bills to be paid. He puts food on my table, when I don't know where my next meal will come from. When I am feeling lonely, He rocks me in his loving arms. When my burdens are seemingly too heavy from me to bear, He lightens my load by taking away the burdens of life. When I can't see my way because my eyes are filled with tears, He wipes my tears away so that I can continue on life's journey. He is a friend when family and friends turn away from me. When I am sick, He comes to see about me. He heals my broken heart and shields me from my enemies. When I am so tried from the issues of this world and can't seem to go a step further, He carries me to the finish line. Jesus is my all and all. Jesus is my Savior. He saved my soul, by suffering and dying on the cross. He did it just for me, so I give my all to Him. Who do you say Jesus Is?

Life is a race and we must run it with all
our might. We can run this race, finish this race
and get our reward because Jesus has done everything necessary of us to endure in our faith.
Jesus is our example and model, for he focused
on the joy that was set before Him. His attention was not on the agonies of the Cross, but
on the crown, not on the suffering, but on His
reward of being able to sit at the right hand of
His Father. While running this Christian race,
we must do as Jesus and stay focus on the prize,
which is eternal life. Don't focus on things you
cannot change, focus on Him. When you come
up against opposition, instead of pondering the
things and the people opposing you, keep your
mind on Jesus Christ and the things of God. Our
Father knows everything you come up against
before you are faced with the situations. If you
set Christ before you and endure, you will have
the victory in the end. When Jesus endured the
cross He did it for the joy that was set before
Him. He looked forward to pleasing His Father
and being able to share the kingdom of God
with us.

In striving for perfection, we need to learn
the principles of discipline. Life is not about doing what we want to do, but it is doing what we
should be doing according to the Word of God.
We must understand that our relationship with
God is the most important relationship that will
ever be afforded to us. Placing the last piece of
the puzzle requires us to make sure everything is

aligned. Being aligned with the word means all that our pieces are in place and we are aligned with our Father's desires for us. When the last piece is in place, a person's life is not the same. The evilness that was allowed to over shadow you in the past can no longer touch you. It can't touch you because Jesus is shielding you from all hurt harm and danger. When the last piece is in place, there is nothing but love in your heart, for everyone that crosses your path. Yes, everyone including your enemies, I must take it a step further and say especially your enemies.

It's the last piece that gives you what you need when you are faced with oppositions. When you place the last piece in the correct spot, your enemies run away from you instead of running to you. Your friends can't stand being around you anymore because they don't understand the change. Just know, it's not you they are running away from. It's the God in you that they can't be around.

When putting together a puzzle, the last piece is very vital because it holds the whole puzzle together. The thing about a puzzle is that I don't care how many pieces you put into place, until the last piece is in place you are constantly putting a piece that has already been placed back in its' place. The pieces are always coming apart. As Christians we can think we have everything in place, but until we've got the last piece in place we are not complete. The last piece is the vital piece because it's got holding power. There is nothing more powerful than the holding power of the love of Jesus Christ. It's the love of Jesus that makes us love everyone. It's the love of Jesus that won't allow us to mistreat anyone. It's the love of Jesus that gives us the strength to keep going through our storms. It's the love of Jesus that speaks to us when we want to give up and encourage us to keep on going. It is the vital piece that can hold that marriage together that appears to be falling apart. The vital piece is what can change the heart of that rebellious child. It's the vital piece that open doors when you think they are all closed, not only closed but padlocked.

The last piece, the vital piece must be in place to complete the puzzle. The last piece, the vital piece must be in place for you to be fully equipped as you strive daily to reach perfection. The last piece is what secures and ensure that you have the love you need to kindred the joy, peace, kindness, forgiving spirit, and endurance to stay in the race until you reach the finish line. It's so important that you reach the finish line because the vital piece has made sure that you get a reward at the end. He died so that you may have eternal life. Eternal life in a place where we will be free, a place where there will be no more pain, no more sorrow, no more suffering, and we won't have to shed another tear. Jesus Christ has prepared a place for us, but we have got to be obedient, striving everyday to live the perfect life in Him. Yes, living a perfect life can be attained, but you must strive daily to reach perfection. The perfect life can only be attained by way of Jesus Christ. I say to you, be encouraged, as you strive daily for perfection in your Christian walk. The vital piece is our Lord and Savior Jesus Christ.

Chapter Ten

THE COMPLETED PUZZLE

I remember being so excited about completing the unusual puzzle I had work so hard on. I was equally excited about the completion of the last chapter of this book. The closer I got to the final chapter the more excited I became. It wasn't long before my excitement turned into disappointment. When I sat down to start the final chapter, I sat and stared at a blank computer screen. Once again I was missing a piece. I purposed in my heart that *Missing Pieces* would be complete in two weeks. There it was two weeks later and *Missing Pieces* is missing a piece. I couldn't believe that I was in this situation again; the last piece is missing. I kept searching my mind, praying for an ending, but God never answered me. Well, I thought, He hadn't answered me. I set the goal of finishing the book in two weeks, because I knew I would be leaving to attend a women's retreat. I was looking forward to returning home and relaxing before I started another project. I shared with a friend that I had to finish the book before we left for the retreat. I explained to her that I did not want to return home working on the same project. She said to me, "Maybe you will not be able to finish before you leave, maybe the end is at the retreat." I still insisted that I was going to complete this book before going to the retreat. Needless to say I have been back from the retreat two days. I am just beginning to write the last chapter.

As I looked back I realized something, look how many times I used the word "I." I forgot something very important. The writing this book had nothing to do with me, but everything to do with God. No, I could not finish when I wanted to because God's time is not my time. I had gotten so caught up in completing the book that I forgot about the one who was truly writing the book. I had to remind myself, everything I do must be for the His glorification, I am only His vessel. On the last day of the retreat, I awoke giving thanks to God, for the blessings He had bestowed upon me during the retreat. It was then He spoke to me and said, "Now you can write the last chapter, the last piece is the retreat." The same words my friend had spoken. The women's ministry mission statement is, "Forsaking all things, proclaiming righteousness." The theme for the retreat was, "Break Through, Break Free." As I pondered the mission statement and the theme it became evident that if we plan to strive for perfection we must break though all our strongholds before we break free. It is then that we will have the right mindset. The right mindset is what gives us an understanding on how to forsake all things, as we can walk in righteousness. The ladies who were in attendance at the retreat were all women who had many things in common. But there were two factors that were important for this retreat. First, they were women of God who knew God and glorified God by working for Him. And secondly, they all had a desire to move into a higher level of service for Him. These ladies came on this retreat with the mindset of seeking God's Will for their lives, so that they would be able to move to a higher level of service. Notice I said before they got to the retreat they had purposed in their mind the things of God and how to better serve Him. They did not get into God's business by telling him what they were going to do. But they waited for God to handle His business by allowing Him to direct them to that higher place.

Every session was a new experience with God. Every session God would reveal himself to us in a different way, every time taking each of us to a higher level of worship. There were times when the anointing flowed through the room, I could only stand and watch in total amazement. The more God revealed himself to us the more we wanted. There were times I wondered why He would not allow His Spirit to completely overtake me. God spoke to me and said, "You are in My Presence. I have taken you to another level, but I need you to be aware of your surroundings because you have a story to tell." After hearing God speak those words, I knew He was preparing me to be used on a much higher level. It was in the midnight hour that He revealed to me that He was not preparing me for another work. He was preparing me to complete the puzzle that was already laid out. God turned on the light and showed me the missing piece. God was taking me to a higher level to be able to continue to do His Work. It's so amazing how God works when He wants to use us. All we have to do is wait on Him as He guides and directs us.

The women's retreat is a yearly event; therefore most of these ladies had been in attendance every year. As planning progressed for this retreat it became obvious to both the retreat coordinator and me that this would be a special retreat. In the past, the retreat was very structured, every event planned as well as every timeframe that everything would to take place. In the past everyone who signed up to attend spoke about being anxious to get away and needing the break from routine. This year there were many who signed up to attend that cancelled out, some even cancelled just a few days before the retreat. I was beginning to get a little concerned because not only were we few in numbers, but no agenda had been put in place. The one thing that was noticeable was the attitudes and the mindset of the few that were planning to attend. In talking to each of them never once did anyone say, "I can't wait to get away," like so many had said in the past. Instead all were saying, "I am excited and ready to receive what God has for me." Even the efficient retreat coordinator, who was only allowed to cover the basic arrangements this year, could only talk about receiving what God had for her to receive. Her focus was not on the small details as in the past years, but renewing the spirit within her and the mindset of moving to a higher level in her walk with God. When I attended church as a child, at the beginning of church service there was an old deacon who would always begin worship service with a saying, "It's time to get you mind stayed on God so we can better serve Him." The ladies who attended the retreat had their mind stayed on God.

We realize that God is in control of everything, but sometimes we forget to let Him be in control. The flesh measures success based on numbers, how many were in attendance, did they all enjoy themselves and how many would be willing to attend the next year. God reminded me where there are two or three gathered in His name, touching and agreeing, He would be in the midst. As I look back, I can see God working in the midst from the beginning, which started at the retreat the preceding year. There were those who attended just to say they went somewhere, those who came bound down with unnecessary baggage but were not willing to leave the baggage behind to make a new start. There were those who realized that they had extra junk in their baggage so they just tucked it back in a safe spot until they returned home. And there were those who came truly seeking God. But don't you know Satan found a way to slip in? But God; the one who was in control, took charge and remove those who not serious about his work. He began to move in the minds and hearts of the ones who wanted to receive him. God started the weeding out process last year and continued the process into the departure for this year. I was concerned with numbers while God was busy convicting those who had a mindset to make a change and move to the next level in their service for Him. The ladies that attended this year were those who were laboring for God in some capacity. There were ministers, evangelists, Sunday school teachers, choir members and ushers in attendance. A representation from all areas of the church, which signifies to us that no matter what duty one assumes as a servant leader; God calls us all to a higher level of service. Also in attendance was a new convert who also had a burning desire in her heart to serve God. She came seeking God for a change of mind and a desire to break the chains that bind her. Everyone came looking to break through to break free.

The foundation was laid in the first session, which started with praise and worship. As we began to praise our Heavenly Father, everyone in the chapel was filled with the Holy Spirit. The anointing was so powerful; some were speaking in tongues, some fell to their knees and yes, some lay on the floor slain in the Spirit. There was one who was as David, praising God as she danced before him in the spirit. This was just the beginning, all minds turned away from their problems, families, finances, sickness and the work place. Our minds were focused on God. I know that God was pleased, after all, we were created to worship and praise him. We prayed, worshiped and studied until God decided to release us from his power. God was the center of everything that was done in those three days. The first day was all about each of us taking at close look at ourselves, no one had time to look at someone else. This was a personal evaluation for everyone in attendance.

The personal evaluation was the first step to putting all the pieces in place. The first things God did was reminded us of who we are. He reminded us that we were his children. Our thoughts had to be changed and the door of the flesh closed. God removed the stronghold of Satan and placed only the thoughts of Jesus Christ in our minds. There was a thirst manifesting among us, a thirst that could not be quenched with water. It was a thirst for the "Living Water," we longed to drink of the living waters because we knew that if we took one drink of the living water we would never thirst again.

> *"For as he thinketh in his heart, so is he,"*
>
> Proverbs 23:7

It was the desire to drink of the living waters that ushered in the change of the mindset. Yes, we acquired the mind of Christ when we were saved, but the thirst to go higher in the service of the Lord took our mindset to a whole new level.

> *"If ye continue in my word, then are ye my disciples indeed; And ye shall know the truth, and the truth shall make you free."*
>
> John 8:31-32

To have a mind of Christ is a wonderful way of life, you act like Him, you think like Him, you love like Him and all your relationships is a pattern of the relationship Jesus have with His Father.

> *"Finally, brothers, whatsoever things are true, whatsoever things are honest, whatsoever things are just, whatsoever*

things are pure, whatsoever things are lovely, whatsoever things are of good report; if there be any virtue, and if there be any praise, think on these things."

Philippians 4:8

Keeping the piece of mindset in place is not an easy task. To protect you new Christ-like mind there are some things we must remember. When thoughts provoked by the flesh begin to seek into your mind turn your thoughts on the Word of God. Pray for God to keep you mind focused on Him. Humble yourself daily before God. Remember keeping the mindset of Christ is not easy, but just as you are tempted Christ was tempted while on this earth also.

"But his delight is in the law of the Lord, and on His law doth he meditate day and night."

Psalms 1:2

Each session was filled with the Holy Spirit. The last session was one of celebration. It was a celebration of victory in Christ. It is not until all the pieces of the puzzle are in place that you can have a victory celebration. Victory means to gain success or to defeat something which means you must be in competition with something or someone. The women of God came to the retreat prepared for battle. They were prepared to defeat Satan. Victory is rewarded only after all of the pieces are in place. And it is only after the conquests are we able to strive daily for perfection.

Once all the proper steps are taken and all the correct pieces are placed in their identifiable spots it is then that the victory can be proclaimed. You may ask the question, "How do I know when all the pieces are accurate?" You will know, because you will be as Ezekiel when he said the Holy Spirit was as fire shut up in his bones. Your victory will be as fire shut up in your bones. In victory you are now filled with the Holy Spirit. Because you have made some changes and have stirred up the desire to live for and to serve the only true and living God.

> *"But now ye also put off all these: anger, wrath, malice, blasphemy, and filthy communication out of your mouth."*
>
> Colossians 3:8

Now that the Holy Spirit is deeply embedded within you, mean you have now gained understanding. It is the Holy Spirit that gives you the understanding of God's Word, because now your mind is opened to the truth. Being filled with the Holy Spirit is what grants you witnessing power as well as a forgiving heart.

"But as it is written; Eye hath not seen, nor ear heard, neither have entered into the heart of man, the things which God hath prepared for them that love him. But god hath revealed to them unto us by his Spirit."

I Corinthians 2:9-10

Being filled with the Holy Spirit brings about changes. The love in you is measured by how much you love God. When the love of God is in your spirit it overflows to everyone around you. It can be seen in the way you walk, the conversations you hold, the ability to act in situation and not react. The decisions you make are based on your love for God. The word "I" is no more your main concern in life.

"Put on therefore, as the elect of God, holy and beloved, bowels of mercies, kindness, humbleness of mind, meekness, longsuffering;"

Colossians 3:12

When the pieces are in place you have a forgiving heart. You now love and pray for your enemies, you feed the poor, reach out to the needy. You surrender your all to God allowing the Holy Spirit to fill your constantly and share the overflow with others. You are controlled by the spirit and sanctified by the spirit.

*"For he whom God hath sent speaketh
the words of God: for God giveth not
the Spirit by measure unto him."*

John 3:34

Victory means that you no longer base
what is right or wrong on what it feels, like. You
now turn away from those worldly views and do
what's right according to God's Word, and recognize sin as sin. God gave us emotions, we are
to control our emotions and not be controlled
by them. God gave us emotions so that we can
have a mixture of feelings. He wants us to experience joy, happiness, love, laughter, pain and
grief. When we are in control of our emotions
we do not allow one of these emotions to take
over our life. Imagine what it would be like to
have the emotion of grief to take control of everything you do, how miserable that would be.
Having a mind of Christ is the key to controlling our emotions. Taking control of your mind,
will, and emotions is what moves you from being a religious person to a true disciple of God.
It is a true disciple, who allows only the Holy
Spirit to control him. Be encouraged my brothers and sisters and press toward the mark, the
mark of perfection.

*"Not as though I had already attained,
either were already perfect: but I follow
after, if that I may apprehend that for*

*which also I am apprehended of Christ
Jesus."*

Take control of your mind and know that
no one can live unequally balanced. If you proclaim to love God, you must walk the walk and
know without a doubt that God is the Almighty
One, the only one worthy of all the praises.
Perfection is earned through hard work, and
gained as you mature spiritually. Yes, because
of the downfall of Adam and Eve, all men are
born sinners. Realizing this and drawing closer
to God, through His Son Jesus Christ, we can
gain perfection.

*"For the law made nothing perfect, but
the bringing in of a better hope did; by
which we draw nigh unto God."*

Hebrews 7:19

*"And being made perfect, he became
the author of eternal salvation unto all
them that obey him."*

Hebrews 5:9

I had an opportunity to be in attendance
in a class, the instructor used a vase to illustrate
why we as humans will never be able to live a
perfect life in Christ. The instructor filled the
vase with paper. She stuffed as much paper in
the vase as possible. She then lifted the vase for

everyone to see. Although she had put as much paper in the vase that it could hold, there were still gaps and spaces that could be seen between the papers. As long as the vase was sitting on the table, the students could only see it from a certain angle therefore the vase appeared to be full. It was not until the vase was held up to the light that the empty spaces became visible to us. The instructor held up the vase and said, the empty spaces you see between the papers represent sin. She went on to say that the vase represented our lives, we can never be perfect because sin is a part of our nature and the spaces can never be filled. The instructor took a second vase and filled it with water; the vase was filled to the rim. She stated that this vase represented what a spirit-filled life should be, but because of the flesh we will never reach this point. I understood the illustrations but God revealed another side of the illustrations to me. What God revealed to me awaken in my heart the fact that we can and must live a life of perfection. If this was an impossible goal to reach God would have never gave us the book of instructions to guide us to the point of perfection.

The first vase was stuffed with paper and yet there were empty spaces. This represented the life of a sinner. This person has lived their entire life believing that their life was fine. It didn't matter that his or her life consisted of lying, stealing, backbiting and adultery. Because on Sunday they made sure they attended church. But one day they came into the true path of Jesus Christ, the light shinned so bright that they could not help be see all of their shortcomings. The gaps and spaces in their life were now revealed. What they thought was right now appears as sin. Once the empty spaces were revealed and the light came on and the sinner recognized he had been living in the dark begin to work to change things. The sinner decided to work to fill the empty spaces. Or rather remove the junk from their life and replace the empty spaces with the pieces that were missing in their life.

The Word of God tells us to be filled with the Holy Spirit, not with junk, but the Holy Spirit. If we replace our sin-sick life with the wholeness of the Holy Spirit we can be nothing but perfect. When the water was poured into the second vase, I saw the sinner changing his life, from a sin filled life to a life filled with the Holy Spirit. When we allow ourselves to be filled with the Holy Spirit there is no room for anything else to vanquish our life. Being filled means there is no opportunity afforded to sin to come in and occupy the empty spaces. I not only saw the vase being filled to the rim but the water overflowing. Because there cannot be boundaries placed when it comes to the flowing of the living waters. When the Holy Spirit fills us the filling continues until it overflows to others.

Putting together puzzles is one of my many hobbies. Another hobby of mine is building things from Lego blocks. I am reminded of a battleship that I build from Lego blocks. I would work on it in stages, being careful to make sure every piece were in the right place. I had just about completed the battleship in fact one more sitting and the battleship would be complete. As least that's what I believed. My son came to visit me for the weekend, he too loves to work with puzzles and Lego blocks. I noticed he picked up the battleship and examined it very close. He would put it down and go back and pick it up again. Finally, he said to me, "Mom, you have one piece that's out of place and it's throwing the whole battleship off." My response to him was that no one would notice and I was going to finish it like it was. He then began to take the battleship apart to correct the piece that was in the wrong place. At first, I was upset but I realized that to be perfect, all the pieces must be in the right place. When he had completed the battleship I could see a difference, all the pieces were in the right place. Just as my son noticed the piece out of place and took it apart to start over again. Sometimes we must do this with our spiritual life. When you notice that because of the trials of life a piece has gotten out of place, open your heart and mind and allow God to direct you to getting the piece back in place. God wants us to be perfect. But we must strive for perfection and work daily to maintain our perfection. As I said earlier, no you cannot do this by yourself this goal can only be attained by the help of God, by way of His son Jesus Christ.

THE ONLY WAY TO REACH PERFECTION IS TO STRIVE FOR PERFECTION. IF YOU DON'T STRIVE FOR PERFECTION YOU WILL NEVER REACH PERFECTION.

CONCLUSION

Striving for perfection means there must be a self examination. To examine something is to look into, in order to get a clearer understanding. The last thing we, as humans, want to do or feel comfortable doing is examining ourselves simply because an examination of one's self can and will uncover some unpleasant facts. Facts that we prefer to keep buried. As humans it is more important to look good to others, rather than standing for what's right according to God's Holy Word. Take some time and examine yourself so that you may know yourself and what's keeping you from reaching perfection. Make sure you first evaluate yourself in truth. Pray for wisdom to accept and understand the things in your life that need to be improved or changed. Who you are is based solely on your relationship with

God. It's important that we know that God will not reveal to us His purpose for our life or who we truly are until we know, trust and have faith in Him. Who are you? Are you living your life based on who you are on your job? Your status in the financial market or your wealth, or are you basing who you are on the position you hold in the church? Look in the mirror, when you look take a look beyond the things that make you look good and search deep to discover who you are and the purpose for which God has placed you on this earth.

> *"Counsel in the heart of man is like deep water; but a man of understanding will draw it out."*
>
> Proverbs 20:5

Are you walking with Christ? Is your walk one filled with the spirit of love, joy, kindness, patience, longsuffering, goodness, faithfulness, gentleness and self-control? If you are not bearing the fruit of the spirit, then you need to reevaluate your walk with Christ.

> *"Mortify therefore your members which are upon the earth; fornication, uncleanness, inordinate, affection, evil concupiscence, and covetousness, which is idolatry,"*
>
> Colossians 3:5

Are you willing to forsake all things? The perfect walk with Jesus is one that does not included material items. It means that we must put aside family, friends and worldly possession and our will so that we are free to life for His purpose. Christ has to be the center of our lives; everything else should revolve around the center, as the branches of a tree. It is prayer and study that will keep you in the place with God, forsaking all others. No, a Christian cannot live the perfect life until they have examined the mind and emptied the evil thoughts and ideas of the world. Emptying your mind will allow God to empower you though your walk with him. You need to know that you are not who others say you are, or what others say about you. You are a child of God empowered by Him to do only the things that He would have you do.

Remember you must have faith to hold all the pieces together. God's Word tells us that "Without faith it is impossible to please Him." Webster's definition of faith is to be convinced, complete trust, confidence, reliance, unquestioning belief that does not require proof and an unquestioning belief in God. Tyndale's Bible Dictionary defines faith as an attitude of complete trust in God. Not a passing fad, but a continuous attitude of trust and belief.

Faith and Hope: Hope is the expectation of good. Therefore, hope is the soil out of which faith grows and keeps faith alive. Faith and Trust: There can be no faith and hope without trust. God is totally trustworthy. As Christians we stand on His promises because we know that He is reliable.

> *"Trust in the Lord with all thine heart; and lean not unto thine own understanding. In all thy ways acknowledge Him and He shall direct thy paths."*
>
> Proverbs 3:5-6

When the pieces of your puzzle are in place, including the vital piece, you will need to make sure it stays together. Take the bonding agent of faith and spread it over the entire puzzle. This will enable you to stay strong as you strive for perfection.

There is a song that is sung in the Black American Baptist Church, a song that dates back to our forefathers. The words of the song say: "Trying to make one hundred, ninety nine and one half won't do. Even our forefathers realized that in order to receive the gift of eternal life we have got to make one hundred, because we can't make it by stopping at ninety nine and one half. I pray that one hundred is your goal.

ALWAYS STRIVE FOR PERFECTION BECAUSE IT CAN BE ATTAINED TO GOD BE THE GLORY!

ABOUT THE AUTHOR

The author, Reverend Gwengale J. Parker, is a woman of God. She attended various Georgia colleges where she obtained a BA in Business Administration and Accounting, and a Masters in Divinity. She is an ordained minister of the gospel of the Baptist faith.

She is the wife of Charles Parker. The mother of three: Marcus, Crystal and DeWayne. The grandmother of two: Crystal and D'Asia.

The author does not see or understand the importance of credentials gained on this earth. Therefore she describes herself as a servant of God, all about doing her Heavenly Father's Will. One who enjoys preaching, teaching the Word of God. And striving to take Christians out of a building called church and put the church where God intended for it to be: in the hearts of men.

The author strives daily to live the life she teach and preach about every day. She gives God the glory for all things.